• A Beginner's Guide •

GOLD...

ABC's OF PANNING !

by E.S. "Rocky" LeGaye

- How To Find Placer Gold
- The Necessary Equipment
- How To Use Your Gold-Pan

FREE   Treasure Reference Catalog

Dealer Discounts Available

Copyright© 1975, by E.S. LeGaye

reprinted by
CARSON ENTERPRISES
Drawer 71, Deming, NM 88031-0071

ISBN 0-941620-03-4

Library of Congress Catalog Card Number: 74-128599

E.S. "Rocky" LeGaye, at Houston, Texas, October, 1972. The beard, pipe, and an optimistic zest for life have been part of me for so long...guess they'll have to stay!

1915-1981

Here is a bit about myself:
Born September 11th, 1915, at San Bernardino, California. Attended grammar school in Calif., high school in Georgia, and college (spread over more years than usual, due to the Depression) in Florida and Texas. Holder of F.C.C. Radiotelephone License, 1st-Class, since 1945; member of Western Writers of America, U.S. National Archives, and 7 historical and historical-research societies. I have worked at all manners of jobs during my life, but there has always been a strong pull to gold mining — especially placering. Since the early 1930's, I have prospected over much of the beautiful, high-mountain Sierra Nevadas...and other places. *Found a bit of gold, too!* During 40 or so years of such doing, one manages to learn how to spot likely places for gold to be, and how best to get it out of the ground and into the gold-poke. But, it isn't only my personal experiences and the teachings of many "old prospector" types that provide me with the technical data necessary for writing my gold books. During those same years, I accumulated what I believe to be one of the finest private libraries on gold and placering to be found anywhere. So... when I need information outside the limits of my own knowledge, I can usually find it in my library, written by practical-minded experts. *Here, then, are the sources of the realistic data I try always to pass on to my readers: personal experience, teachings of successful miners, and authoritative textbooks.*

GOLD AND HIGH ADVENTURE ARE PARTNERS...inseparably linked together by the legends out of our ancient, misty past. Singly — or together — they possess the power to stir mens' souls and to spur them on to fantastic feats. The legends bear eloquent testimony that this is so...and as long as men of courage are born, it shall always be so!

FOREWORD

ROSPECTING AND PANNING FOR GOLD in the streams of the West can make you rich beyond belief! Well, perhaps not rich in gold...but rich, certainly, in health and peace of mind, and in an awakened sense of oneness with your Creator. It can give you a sense of richness of adventure and thrills that never grow old. If you are a beginner at prospecting and panning, if you have not yet felt that build-up of emotional expectancy that comes to nearly everyone (including the professionals!), as you work your pan down nearer to the bottom (down where the gold — if any – is about to show), then you have something truly wonderful ahead of you. *It is one of Life's unforgettable first-time experiences...when, suddenly, you see your own gold in your own pan!*

And when you find your first real nugget...*hoo, boy!* Let me tell you, no matter how much money you make, no matter how much cold cash you have in the bank...when you actually see that first golden nugget in your pan -- that beautiful, priceless treasure that you have personally wrested from the jealous grasp of Mother Nature -- why, *at that moment, you suddenly feel at least nine feet tall!*

And that night, as you sit beside your campfire, you'll carefully take your nugget out and look at it again...and heft it a bit from time to time, even if it does only weigh a quarter of an ounce! Soon you'll likely find your thoughts beginning to drift — lazily -- with tantalizing images crossing your mind: Glimpses of the Old West...yes, 49'ers working with gold pans and sluice box strings; Wells Fargo stages and iron-bound treasure boxes; grim-visaged guards armed with six-guns and shotguns, and even grimmer-visaged outlaws armed with six-guns and rifles; poker-faced gamblers and painted-face dance-hall hurdy gurdy girls; grizzled desert-rat prospectors trailing out across lonely wastes, followed by their patient burro-companions; and *gold, Gold, GOLD!* Leather pokes full of gold dust and nuggets, express company boxes full of gold bars...and buried caches full of bright, beautiful gold coins!

Yes, a visualized panorama of life out of the the misty past will surround this moment with a magic mantle...to fill your heart and spirit with a pervasive nostalgia for those lusty yesteryears and stir a quickening sense of anticipation for tomorrow. As you sit there by your flickering campfire, utterly bewitched by this moment, you will begin to hear the sweet call of a siren-song more fascinating, more compelling than anything you've ever before experienced. And you will be eager to answer!

My friend...*you have just come down with Gold-Fever!*

Is this really too bad? Look at it this way: Psychologists tell us that people quickly grow old — far beyond their actual years — when they can no longer be enthusiastic about their activities, when they no longer feel a gusto for the affairs of their daily living...and, most important, when they lose hope for the future. Objective observation forces me to agree with the psychologists in this conclusion...as tragic examples — semi-living proofs — are to be found everywhere about you. Just look...and you will see!

This being so, then let me tell you...*panning for gold is better than a Fountain of Youth for keeping you vibrantly alive in body and young in heart!* The outdoor living puts a spring into your step and a glow into your cheeks. The prospecting and panning for gold puts a zesty enthusiasm into your spirit and a yeasty, bubbling expectancy into your emotions. And, as for hope, well...regardless of the disappointment in *this* pan, there is always the *next* pan...or the one after *that*, for sure! When one crevice has been carefully cleaned out...there is always another one even more promising, right across the stream! Yes, there is always another gravel bar on up ahead — or another stream — where the air is fresh and sparkling-clear, the water cool and sweet.

So...*Viva la Gold-Fever!*

Now, one more point: While you might never find more than better health, renewed enthusiasm for living, and a revitalized hope for the future... there is always the very real chance that you will find a "Glory-Hole" filled with gold. Others have, so, *why not you!*

CONTENTS GOLD...ABC's of Panning!

THIS BOOK IS ONE OF A SERIES by E.S. "Rocky" LeGaye, about the resources, people and events that helped create our great "Western Heritage" and the reality of a bountiful America that does indeed stretch "...*from sea to shining sea.*" In spite of their very human failings, those valiant souls brought into being in this land conditions and opportunities that have instilled more hope and answered more dreams for more people — for a longer period of time — than any other group in any other land since the dawn of recorded history.

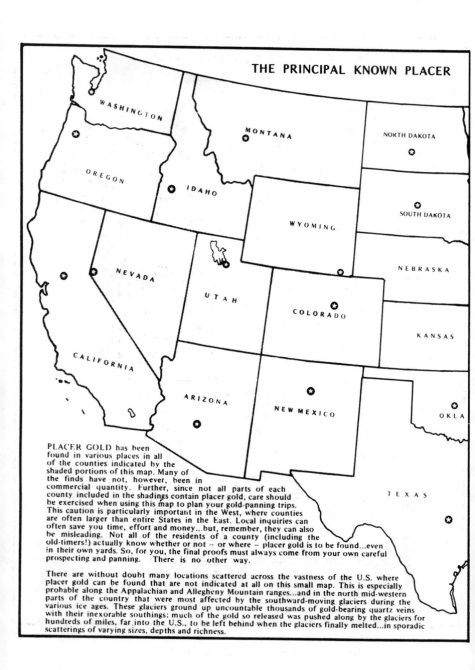

THE PRINCIPAL KNOWN PLACER

WASHINGTON

OREGON

MONTANA

NORTH DAKOTA

IDAHO

SOUTH DAKOTA

WYOMING

NEBRASKA

NEVADA

UTAH

COLORADO

KANSAS

CALIFORNIA

ARIZONA

NEW MEXICO

OKLA

TEXAS

PLACER GOLD has been found in various places in all of the counties indicated by the shaded portions of this map. Many of the finds have not, however, been in commercial quantity. Further, since not all parts of each county included in the shadings contain placer gold, care should be exercised when using this map to plan your gold-panning trips. This caution is particularly important in the West, where counties are often larger than entire States in the East. Local inquiries can often save you time, effort and money...but, remember, they can also be misleading. Not all of the residents of a county (including the old-timers!) actually know whether or not -- or where -- placer gold is to be found...even in their own yards. So, for you, the final proofs must always come from your own careful prospecting and panning.   There is no other way.

There are without doubt many locations scattered across the vastness of the U.S. where placer gold can be found that are not indicated at all on this small map. This is especially probable along the Appalachian and Allegheny Mountain ranges...and in the north mid-western parts of the country that were most affected by the southward-moving glaciers during the various ice ages. These glaciers ground up uncountable thousands of gold-bearing quartz veins with their inexorable southings; much of the gold so released was pushed along by the glaciers for hundreds of miles, far into the U.S., to be left behind when the glaciers finally melted...in sporadic scatterings of varying sizes, depths and richness.

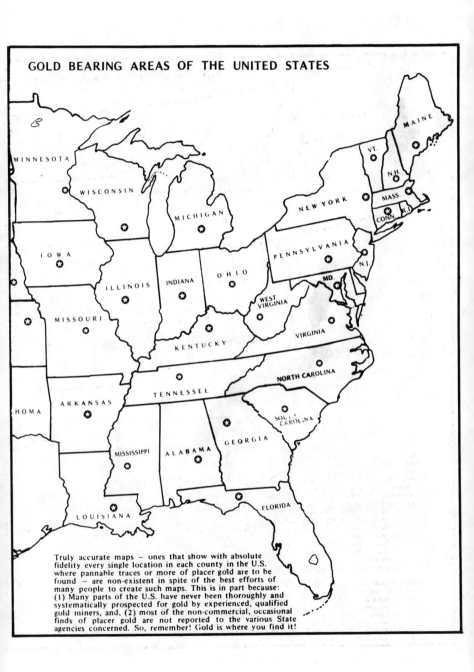

GOLD BEARING AREAS OF THE UNITED STATES

Truly accurate maps — ones that show with absolute fidelity every single location in each county in the U.S. where pannable traces or more of placer gold are to be found — are non-existent in spite of the best efforts of many people to create such maps. This is in part because: (1) Many parts of the U.S. have never been thoroughly and systematically prospected for gold by experienced, qualified gold miners, and, (2) most of the non-commercial, occasional finds of placer gold are not reported to the various State agencies concerned. So, remember! Gold is where you find it!

THE METAL CALLED GOLD

The How And Why Of Your Interest In It

THERE IS LITTLE DOUBT that gold was the first metal to be utilized by Man, far back in the distant remoteness of his prehistoric past. He most likely found it then as it is still being found...amongst the river sands and gravels, in little bits and pieces, and occasionally, in chunks as large as his hand. The brightly shining grains of metal attracted his attention, and he found pleasure in picking them up and playing with them. He learned to tie the bits together with pieces of leather, and in so doing, he created the first jewelry...bracelets and necklaces. He later discovered ways to work the metal into shapes and forms of his own chosing...first by pounding, stretching and twisting, and later, by melting and casting.

Slowly, through the centuries, he learned to make other things with this strange, pretty substance. Not only simple bracelets and necklaces, but anklets and other pieces of jewelry, dishes, bowls, pitchers, goblets and eating utensils. During this same period of time, he came to find that his golden trinkets could be exchanged for many things that he needed in his daily living. Because gold was scarce even then, and because his metal working labor was tedious and time consuming...the golden objects of his craftsmanship gained a positive utility value, and so, a price.

By the year 5000 B.C., working with gold had become an art. By 4000 B.C., man had virtually mastered the metal and was now making intricate, beautiful pieces of jewelry, lavish decorations and exquisitely detailed idols shaped into the images of his various and many gods. During this time, gold had become quite valuable...too much so to be allowed to the common men who found, mined and worked it. Gold was now not only the tangible, negotiable wealth of the priesthood and ruling class, it was the primary symbol of power...and means of retaining that power. Gold was used to pay for equipping and maintaining armies, for the building of great temples and elaborate burial-places...and it was also used quite often for paying tribute to conquerors.

Wherever gold was to be found, common men were enslaved and forced — with threats of the whip, dismemberment and death — to toil away their lives in extracting it from the earth and working it into forms desired by their masters. Over a period of many centuries, countless tens of thousands of these unfortunate, cruelly-exploited human beings were sacrificed every year...in order that the gleaming yellow metal could be piled ever-higher in the treasure houses of the priests and rulers. *And it was!*

Slowly time passed by, century following century. The miserable fate of the slave-miners remained the same, however. For them, time was simply labor and pain. They continued to toil away their lives in the service of their "masters"...adding to the golden piles bit by bit, piece by piece and object by object. By the year 1000 B.C., these piles had grown so huge that they were worth incredible fortunes. For example, it has been estimated by historians that David and Solomon — the Second and Third Kings of Israel — accumulated the well-nigh unbelievable amount of eight to ten million pounds, avoirdupois, of gold *(worth between four and five billion dollars, at $35 per troy ounce!)*. This gold was not intended to improve the lot of their people, of course, but to pay for the fabulous Temple, at Jerusalem.

The "human-cost" of this one project alone staggers the imagination...with its countless tragedies of enslavement, of torture and pain, of hunger, sickness, injuries and death. And when multiplied by the vast numbers of other such monuments to Man's egotism, greed and fears, the price of this ancient gold is utterly appalling when considered in terms of human misery. Add to this, the savage despoilings of Africa and Asia Minor by the Egyptians, Arabs, Greeks and Romans, the slave-labor cadres of the cruel Mongolian Khans, the rape of the Americas by the Spaniards and Portuguese, of Indonesia by the Dutch... and all the rest of the brutal predations committed by the hordes of unconscionable exploiters and looters who have marched heavy-footed across the pages of Man's history. The total cost of supporting "supermen" — by common men — has been so incredibly great that one wonders that we have not come to loathe every particle of that gold...so cruelly amassed during those long, dark centuries. *But, we have not!*

It was to be nearly 1800 years after Christ, the gentle teacher of Bethlehem, was crucified before the slave-miners were to become, for the most part, a thing of the past...a part of the darker side of Man's history. The great gold rush to California in 1849 was probably the first time in 60 or 70 centuries that even to the lowliest amongst them, large numbers of free men could aspire to the attainment of personal wealth by mining gold for themselves alone! This inspiration led men from all over the world into making the long, dangerous journey to the California goldfields...55,000 by the overland trails and 25,000 by sea, in 1849 alone!

The idea of searching for one's own gold...of finding one's own personal *El Dorado*, swept like a flame across the entire world. It ignited the imaginations of the courageous, the adventurous, wherever they were in the world... and burned with the fierceness of an unchecked prairie fire. *This was not for slave-miners! This was an enterprise for free men!*

The gold rush to California was followed by one to Nevada, in 1858; to Colorado, in 1859; Idaho and Montana, in the '60s; Dakota Territory, in the '70s; Australia and the Transvaal, in the '80s; and Alaska, in 1898. These prospecting and mining ventures were each different than those of the dismal early centuries; the men involved were not slaves, were not the chattels of any man or group of men. They had that most precious of all private possessions, the power of individual choice...*freedom!* They worked for themselves or for others, and they worked singly or in groups...as they themselves chose. And they were secure in the knowledge that the fruits of their labors would come to themselves to dispose of — wisely or foolishly — as they themselves saw fit.

And I tell you, those free men certainly made their mark upon the world! *During the past 125 or so years — with the assistance of the machinery and processes they developed — they discovered and mined out more gold than was mined throughout all the hundreds of earlier centuries!*

Because of its impact upon his life, for good as well as for evil, there is no wonder that gold has so completely fascinated Man for so long. And this fascination is still as strong as ever...in spite of the fact that hundreds of thousands of men have been enslaved for it, and that equal numbers have been "enslaved" by their compulsions to seek it!

A compulsion is itself a form of slavery...and the compulsion to seek, find and possess gold has sent men to the four corners of the earth searching for it. Compelled, they have sought *(and still seek!)* gold in steamy, tropical jungles, in parched deserts, in remote and rugged mountain fastnesses, and in bitter-cold arctic wastelands. Gold has compelled men to leave their jobs, homes and families...to take the greatest of personal risks for the barest possibilities of personal gain.

And, in addition to its power to compel, gold also possesses an almost-magical power to attract...to lure and seduce with the sweet-voiced songs of a bewitching, beautiful enchantress! Gold has thus lured many men to great suffering, to starvation, and to death from violent causes. For the most part, it has led those who sought only gold's wealth to disappointment and discouragement. But, you must also remember...*gold has led some men to fame, fortune and power!*

Yes, gold and high adventure are truly partners...inseparably tied together by the legends out of our past! Singly or together, they possess the power to stir mens' souls and to spur them to fantastic feats. The legends bear eloquent testimoney that this is so...and as long as men of courage are born, it shall always be so! It is completely natural for you to dream of adventure...

especially whenever adventure doesn't play a large role in your day-to-day existence. And, it is part of your heritage – your birthright – to dream boldly of golden treasure and of riches to be had for the taking!

So, as you read this book, do let yourself dream...of gold-laden mountain streams, of beautiful green forests, bright blue skies and peaceful shady glades, of air so clean it seems to sparkle like crystal. See yourself – in your mind's eye – seated by the cool water, shaded and comfortable. Now, *see yourself panning for gold, at the stream's edge. And see – clearly – big, beautiful nuggets of gleaming, yellow gold, right there, in your pan!* Now, you reach into the pan and pick them out. You rub them with your fingers and feel the good, solid smoothness and weightiness...and you are proud of your accomplishment, you are contented and happy, you are at peace with yourself and with the world!

There! Visualizing this pleasant scene wasn't so hard, was it? By this sort of positive dreaming – a directed form of mental imagery – you can change what up until now might have been a mere possibility into a state of high probability. To attain what you want – whatever it might be – first you must dream. Then, visualize your dream in your mind's eye as being an actuality. By such dreaming – *by dreaming boldly* – of adventure and of gold, you are following in your ancestors' footsteps. Yes, you are claiming your natural birthright to live your life with and for purposes of your own choosing...with enthusiasm!

The Nature Of Gold

GOLD IS A METALLIC ELEMENT...one of the 92 "natural" elements which occur throughout the world. It is one of the few metals which occur in both free-metal and chemically-combined forms...although chemically-combined gold is far more rare than the free-metal or native gold form. The chemical symbol for gold is "Au"...which is taken from the Latin word, *aurum*, which means "shining dawn". The old Romans knew what they were doing when they gave this name to gold! As a shining dawn is one of Nature's loveliest sights, so too, is gold a lovely sight to behold!

Pure and near-pure gold is a lustrous, bright-yellow color when in mass. But when ground into tiny particles, it may be black, purple or ruby-red... depending upon purity and particle size. Gold is a soft metal, having a hardness range of 2.5 to 3.0 Mohs...a bit harder than lead (1.5 Mohs), about the same as copper (2.0 to 2.9 Mohs), and much softer than platinum (4.3 Mohs). The atomic weight of gold is 197.2; its atomic number is 79, with valence 1 or 3. The melting point is 1945.4 degrees Fahrenheit (1063 degrees Centigrade); the boiling point is 4712 degrees Fahrenheit (2600 degrees Centigrade).

Pure gold is very dense (and therefore heavy)...having a specific gravity of 19.32 times the weight of an equal volume of water at 63.5 degrees Fahrenheit. Pure gold weighs 1204.8 pounds, avoirdupois (1464.17 lbs., troy) per cubic foot, or, 0.69722 pounds, avoir. (0.84732 lbs., troy) per cubic inch. As found in the native state, the specific gravity of both placer and lode gold varies widely, due to the presence of lighter metals alloyed with the gold. Where large amounts of copper (sp. gr. 8.30–8.95) and silver (sp. gr. 10.42–10.53) accompany raw gold, the specific gravity of the resultant alloy may be as low as 12.5 (weighing about 780 lbs., avoir.)...but with the metal still looking like gold.

Only the following natural metals are heavier than gold: Platinum (sp. gr. 21.37; 1334.1 lbs., avoir. per cubic foot), iridium (sp. gr. 22.42; 1399.1 lbs., avoir. per cubic foot), and osmium (sp. gr. 22.5; 1404.6 lbs., avoir. per cubic foot). Tungsten is the next lighter metal (sp. gr. 18.6–19.1; 1161.1–1192.4 lbs., avoir. per cubic foot. By comparison, lead is quite light (sp. gr. 11.34; 708 lbs., avoir. per cubic foot), and iron is a real flyweight in comparison with gold (sp. gr. 7.85–7.88; 490.1–491.9 lbs., avoir. per cubic foot).

Pure gold is the most malleable of all metals...which means that it can be easily hammered and rolled into various shapes, forms, and thin sheets. Using simple, age's-old gold-beaters' techniques and skills, it is relatively easy (even though a laborious process!) to hammer one ounce of gold into a foil thin enough to cover an area 100 feet square with a sheet of solid gold...about 1/360,000th of an inch thick. *Imagine! Gold plate so incredibly thin that a pile of 360,000 individual sheets will only be one inch high!* Gold this thin easily transmits light...imparting a greenish hue to it. Using modern refinements of the old techniques, films of solid gold as thin as three or four millionths of an inch are easily produced. Such films are used for many purposes, including solar heat reflection and decorations.

Pure gold is also the most ductile (stretchable) of all metals. One troy ounce can be drawn out into a piece of wire 45 to 60 miles long, depending upon die quality and temperature control. This is a mighty long piece of wire — even if exceedingly thin — to pull from a pellet of metal less that 1/10th of a cubic inch in volume (approximately 15/32's of an inch square). But, even more incredibly, that same one ounce of gold could also be used to plate a very thin strand of copper or silver wire 1000 miles long!

Few elements on earth are as stable chemically (and therefore imperishable) as gold. While it is both univalent and trivalent, gold is relatively inactive, chemically, and because of this fact it forms but few compounds. Some substances do react with gold...telluric and selenic acids, for example, plus bromine, chlorine, and calcium, sodium and potassium cyanides, etc. A mixture of 1 part nitric acid to 3 parts hydrochloric acid will readily dissolve gold...for which fact this solution is called *aqua regia*. Because of its stable, non-perishable qualities, gold has long been called a "noble" metal...and noble it is! With few exceptions, a gold coin, ingot or artifact dug up out of the earth or recovered from the sea looks as bright and as lustrous — and is as valuable — as the day it was minted, poured, or crafted!

Pure gold is usually designated as being "1000-fine" (100%) gold. 75% pure gold is 750-fine; 50% pure gold is 500-fine, etc. This is an accurate, easy-to-use method of describing purity, as it uses direct decimal percentages. For example, a piece of gold classified by assay test as being 927-fine would contain 927/1000 parts (92.7%) of pure gold and 73/1000 parts (7.3%) of other metals. Jewelers use a different system to describe purity. In this system, each 1 part of 24 parts is considered to be 1 carat. Thus, in this system, 24-carat gold is 100% pure (1000-fine); 18-carat gold is 75% pure; 12-carat gold is 50% pure, etc.

Without doubt, the metric system of weights will one day become standard throughout the entire world for the weighing of gold. But in the mean-while, the system most used for gold is the troy ounce and pound...which is somewhat different than the avoirdupois system we are accustomed to using in our everyday lives. In the troy system, there are 12 ounces to each troy pound...instead of 16, as in the avoirdupois system. A troy ounce weighs more than an avoirdupois ounce, but an avoirdupois pound weighs more than a troy pound. *Confusion is the word!* Tables for converting from one system to the other are included in this book, beginning on page 78.

In the following way at least, gold can be considered a very haughty metal: *It is extremely choosy in its mating!* Of all the minerals and metals in the world, only the relatively-scarce, semi-metallic element called tellurium is good enough for gold actually to combine with in a true mating. Gold isn't nearly as fussy about mere associates, however. In fact it mixes quite casually and readily with many minerals and metals...accepting them both as impurities and as alloys. These associations include silver, copper, mercury, the platinum group metals, lead, zinc, iron, bismuth, sulfur, etc.

Because of its matings and associations, gold is never found 100% pure in the native state. It is invariably alloyed with one or more other metals and minerals. The ratios of gold to alloying materials -- and their types and indi-vidual quantities -- vary widely from gold field to gold field. But, at the same time, ratios of alloying mixtures tend to remain fairly stable or fixed for each field. These ratios provide, thereby, a sort of metallic "fingerprint" that often can be used to identify the area from which an individual lot of gold comes.

Placer gold is nearly always of a higher purity than lode gold, even in the same producing areas. This comes about as the result of the relatively imperishable nature of gold...in relationship with the less permanent qualities of the accompanying, alloying metals and mineral contaminates. Sulfides leach out, silver and copper both oxidize, etc., leaving the residual gold purer as the result of the losses.

Much South American and Mexican lode gold assays less than 40% pure, with silver being the principal alloying metal. Such an alloy -- 40% or less of gold, with the balance being silver -- is generally called *electrum*, and was once thought to be a metal in its own right...until the Romans succeeded in creating it by alloying gold and silver together. Most of the rest of South American and Mexican raw gold runs no more than 65% to 75% pure...with both silver and copper as principal alloying metals. Nearly all of the gold from California's placers runs 90% pure and better, as does the placer gold in parts of New Mexico...especially the Hillsboro—Gold Dust areas. Much placer gold

E.S. LeGaye: 1962

Wayne Fieldhouse, the writer's nephew, panning gold in Black Canyon, Placer County, California. The site is just downstream from the old New Basel Consolidated drift placer mine which was operated by the writer's great-grandfather, F. de LeGaye, during the 1870's. Most of the gold found in the gravels of Black Canyon came from two underground channels, the New Basel and the Whiskey Hill. These obtained their loadings of gold eons earlier, when they cut through an even older river system called the Blue Lead.

E.S. LeGaye: 1966

Gold from Glenn Edghill's underground placer drift mine, located near the headwaters of Black Canyon, Placer County. Some of the most unusual nuggets this writer has ever seen came from this mine...truly beautiful specimens worthy of the most critical collector.

E.S. LeGaye: 1962

Hope springs eternal with each shovelful of gold-bearing gravel put into pan or sluice box! The writer's son Dan, and Wayne Fieldhouse, using a prospector's sluice in the rugged, remote depths of Big Secret Canyon, Placer County. Such boxes must be used with care.

from British Columbia runs 95% to 98% pure...and one small section in Australia produces placer gold assaying 99.5% pure!

Raw gold destined for coinage, bullion, jewelry, industry, etc., is separated from the accompanying alloy metals and mineral impurities by refining...a process or processes utilizing intense heat, chemicals and electricity. After refining, gold loses its individuality; all pure gold is exactly alike regardless of source or age. Because of practical reasons — mainly involving time and cost — very little gold is ever refined to more than 995-fine. Even the difference between 995-fine and 998-fine can double the refining costs. And, depending upon the alloying metals, refining to 1000-fine could easily cost nearly as much as the gold itself.

Refined gold is usually cast into ingots weighing from several or more ounces up to as much as 80 troy pounds. Most of the gold used in international trade is cast into ingots that weigh 27½ troy pounds. When cast for such use, each ingot bears a weight and fineness stamp, plus the stamp of the refinery that cast and certified the purity of the ingot. The unstamped — and therefore uncertified — ingots and cones often unearthed by today's treasure hunters were usually cast originally by individual miners and small-mill operators for their own convenience in handling. The weight and purity of such unmarked gold varies widely...from as low as 40% gold to perhaps 95% gold.

Gold is so soft and wears away so rapidly it is nearly always intentionally re-alloyed with selected, other metals. This not only gives gold better strength and wear-resistance, it can also change the resultant color of the alloy. The addition of silver, platinum and nickel produces whitish gold; silver and cadmium produce green; copper, pink to red; iron, a bluish tint. U.S. gold coins were 91667-fine from 1792 until 1837, when the purity was cut to 900-fine. Today? Well, we have printing-press "money" — paper currency — unbacked by anything more tangible than public faith in what it will buy on the market place, and we have base-metal, laminated tokens that masquerade in the place of honest coins. Both are monetary travesties, shabby frauds of little or no intrinsic value at all. It is historical fact that currency debasement has preceded every nation's collapse. Are we somehow so different, so wise, that we shall remain immune and escape history's lessons? I hope it to be so with all my heart...even though I cannot believe it with my mind.

Gold Finds: Past, Present And Future

GOLD HAS BEEN FOUND on every continent on earth and in most nations...in more or less amounts. In the U.S., there are but few States where not even a trace has been found...and many States have enough placer gold deposits to make the prospecting and panning both fun and profitable. But, gold is by no means always easy to find, even when you know what you are doing! It is usually distributed thinly, well mixed with appalling tonnages of earth, sand, gravel and rock. To further complicate the finding, gold often occurs as sub-microscopic particles that are totally invisible even when viewed with powerful microscopes.

But, fortunately for the early-day seekers, it also occurs in surprisingly large chunks of solid metal...some of which weigh hundreds of pounds! The largest and greatest number of such "super-nuggets" have come from California and Australia, with Russia and Chile each contributing a few.

Any listing of such massive chunks of gold makes interesting reading...but should be approached with caution and many mental reservations. Remember, reliable records involving events that occur in remote places are difficult to obtain, even today. When you add remote time, the problems multiply logarithmically; the more remote the time, the more the problems. Verifiable records involving gold finds of the last century are certainly no exceptions! And much further confusion has been added through the years by both carelessness and ignorance in the mixing of troy and avoirdupois systems when determining nugget weights. For example, a nugget weighing a true ten troy pounds can become 160 ounces instead of 120 ounces (on paper, by intermixing systems). The next writer decides to convert back to pounds, so divides 160 by 12 troy ounces...to produce (again, on paper) a 13.34 pound nugget. Do this a few more times and see how "big" the nugget gets! In my own research work, I always try to get back to the earliest records, in an attempt to minimize such stretchings.

The largest verified nugget ever found was the *"Ryer & Haultmus"* nugget, discovered in 1872, at Hill End, New South Wales, Australia. This irregular, massive slab of gold was said to be 4'-9" long, 3'-2" wide, and up to 4" thick in parts. It weighed 640 troy pounds (526.6 avoir. lbs.), or, 7680 troy ounces! It assayed 938-fine, and at $19.40 per ounce, it brought almost $149,000! It was reported that the two men who found it were badly in debt — really down on their luck and about to quit — when the chance lucky stroke of a pick raised them from dire poverty to great wealth! *This is the sort of story that lures us on and on...when common sense could otherwise easily dictate a halt!* Even common sense can't always compete with gold!

A few of the other verified large nuggets found in Australia during the 1800's were: the *"Sarah Sands"*, 2688 ounces; the *"Welcome Stranger"*, 2516 ounces; the *"Welcome"*, 2195 ounces; the *"Blanche Barkley"*, 1752 ounces; the *"Precious"*, 1630 ounces; the *"Leg o' Mutton"*, 1620 ounces; the *"Louisa Creek"*, 1272 ounces; the *"Lady Hotham"*, 1188 ounces; the *"Burrondong"*, 1182 ounces; and the *"Viscount Canterbury"*, 1104 ounces. The cumulative total weight of the 15 largest verified Australian nuggets was 28,151 troy ounces (1930.3 avoir. lbs.), an average of 1876.7 ounces (128.7 avoir. lbs.) each. With an average purity of about 940-fine, they brought more than $545,000 to the finders.

The largest verified nugget ever found in the U.S. was the *"Castle Ravine"* nugget. It was found in July of 1853 by John Dodge, on a claim in Castle Ravine, a few miles distant from Downieville, California. The nugget, as originally found, included many small, attached fragments of quartz. When cleaned, the nugget weighed 2724 troy ounces (186.8 avoir, lbs.), and at $18 per ounce, it brought Dodge and his two partners $49,000.

Another nugget — much larger than the *"Castle Ravine"* — was reportedly discovered near Downieville, in 1856...the *"James Finney"* nugget. This report cannot be verified and contains certain doubtful aspects, so I do not include it in my statistics. Here are the alleged "details": James Finney located the nugget on August 21st, 1856, on a claim close to Downieville. It weighed 426.7 troy pounds, or, 5120 troy ounces. Approximately 870-fine, it was sold to the banking firm of Decker & Jewett for $87,500. This firm, in turn, sent the nugget to Philadelphia...where they exhibited it to the public and then sold it to the U.S. Mint for $92,000. If factual, the *"James Finney"* would be the world's second-largest found nugget. There are, however, three major flaws in this story. They are: 1) The story cannot be verified, in spite of the richness of "details" given. 2) In spite of its unusual size and great value, there is not one single mention of the nugget in any historical reference works written before 1890 — when it suddenly burst onto the scene — some 34 years after the alleged finding and public exhibition. And, 3) James Finney existed. He was a well-known, well-written-about prospector and miner of that period, in both California and Nevada. There is nothing in the records that indicate Finney ever in his life had in his hands such a sum as $87,500.

But many large nuggets actually were found in California gold placers during the 1800's...mostly in Calaveras, Tuolumne and Sierra Counties. The 10 largest were: The *"Castle Ravine"*, 2724 troy ounces; the *"Graves Bros."*,

2366 ounces; the *"Calaveras"*, 2289 ounces; the *"Honeycomb"*, 1906 ounces; the *"Monumental Mine"*, 1898 ounces; the *"Jarvis"*, 1584 ounces; the *"China-man's Nugget"*, 1476 ounces; the *"Rattlesnake Creek"*, 1274 ounces; the *"Oliver Martin"*, 1248 ounces (found by Oliver Martin in 1854, while digging a dead friend's grave...near Camp Corona, in Tuolumne County); and the *"Rainbow Mine"*, 1153 ounces. A total of 17,918 troy ounces!

The cumulative total weight of the 25 largest verified California nuggets was 30,444 troy ounces (2087.6 avoir. lbs.) They brought their various finders about $537,000. The individual weights ranged from a top of 2724 ounces to a low of 648 ounces. The cumulative total of the next 50 largest verified California nuggets was 16,665 troy ounces (1142.7 avoir. lbs.). This group ranged from a top of 552 ounces to a low of 146 ounces...and sold for almost $295,000. The cumulative total of this entire group of 75 California nuggets -- mostly found between 1850 and 1880 -- was 47,109 troy ounces (3230.3 avoir. lbs., an average of 43.1 lbs. each). The total reported value was $831,250. But...*at the June, 1974, free-market price-quote of $167 per troy ounce, those 75 nuggets would have brought $7,867,200 to their finders!*

In addition to large nuggets, gold has been found occasionally in huge quantities of small bits and pieces...in both placer deposits and decomposed quartz seams. For example, three sailors mined a claim near Murderer's Bar, on the American River, in 1850. The first day, they hit a rich pocket and took out 29 troy pounds of gold. Within a month, they had extracted more than 500 pounds of dust and nuggets from their claim...about $100,000 worth at the prices then paid. In April, 1851, a man named Contreras is said to have washed 28 pounds of gold out of a hole less than four feet square...in Sullivan's Gulch, near Sonora. Within the first few days of October, 1853, a small group of miners who called themselves the Allegheny Company washed 36 pounds of gold out of their claim at Texas Bar, on the Yuba River. And with only a small rocker, the group known as the Wisconsin Tunnel Company washed out 6¼ pounds of gold from their claim near Iowa Hill...in one day, April 3, 1855.

At a gravel bar near Sonora, more than 3300 ounces of gold were taken from one bedrock area of only 50 square feet...about 66 ounces per square foot! Even at the $17.75 per ounce price then common to the area, the yield was about $58,600...or, $1175 per square foot! And one great lump of com-bined gold and silver found deep within the massive Comstock Lode, at Virginia City, Nevada, yielded something over $105,000,000...at the prices then prevailing!

Admittedly, very few of today's Argonauts are apt to discover such rich spots or such large nuggets...but the fact still remains that the old-timers didn't get it all by any means. They certainly missed a lot of good gold, as the scuba divers and small-dredge operators have discovered! But the lesson for weekend panners and amateur prospectors should be obvious: *When you're hunting bear, hunt where bears have been found. And, if you're hunting big bears, hunt where big bears have been found!*

With but one important exception, the deposits of sub-microscopic gold — often called colloidal gold — apparently offer the richest remaining gold reserves in the U.S., and perhaps in the world. Excellent examples of such deposits are the Carlin and Cortez sites, in Nevada, and an area near Jackson Hole, Wyoming. The Carlin Mine is now the 2nd largest gold producer in the U.S., with ores that are relatively rich for the open-pit mining method involved...but far too poor for conventional shaft and tunnel mining. Carlin ores average somewhat more than 3/10ths of an ounce of gold per ton of ore...but another 9 or 10 tons of worthless overburden must be removed for each ton of ore recovered. But...the Carlin Mine is rich enough that it paid back its entire $10,000,000 initial capital outlay, and the $20,000,000 operating expense, within four years after start-up. In the process, the men and machines at Carlin moved more than 20 million tons of earth and rock... enough to build 3½ Great Pyramids of Egypt!

Even the largest particles of gold in the Carlin Mine ore must be magnified at least 1000 diameters to be seen...and 90% of the particles are smaller than 1/25,000th of an inch in size, completely invisible even under a 1500-power microscope! Such minute particles add up, however, when the volume is great enough. Recently, 50 cubic miles of colloidal gold ore have been mapped, near Jackson Hole, Wyoming. With an assay evaluation of some 300,000,000 troy ounces of gold, this one deposit contains more gold than all the rest ever mined in the U.S., and virtually none of this gold can be seen with the unaided eye! This would be a good place for anyone with a spare 20 or 25 million dollars to begin a profitable mining career.

Gold has been sought and mined by uncounted tens of thousands of men, and it has been stored away for many centuries...over fifty, for sure. But the actual physical smallness of the volume of mined gold — both raw and refined — is amazing when you stop to consider the great effort and expense that has been poured into prospecting, mining, milling, refining and working this metal. The world's entire stock of mined gold is currently estimated to be some 80,000 metric tons — about 176,000,000 avoir, lbs. — and worth, at $35 per troy ounce, perhaps 85 billion dollars. Yet...this entire stock, if brought together into a single pile, would only make a stack 15 feet high, 60 feet wide, and 163 feet long...roughly the volume of a cube somewhat less than 53 feet square!

The one, single greatest depository of unmined gold in the world is the sea, which contains gold in both solution and colloidal forms...and it is to the sea Man must someday turn, when his needs for metals and minerals increase beyond the land's capacity to provide! Numerous processes to recover this sea-borne gold have been tried, some with considerable success. But, to date, all have proven too costly in relationship with the current prices of gold. The man who invents a practical, economically-feasible method of extracting this sea-borne gold can easily become the very richest man on earth.

As is usual in new areas of scientific learning, various researchers find and report differing amounts of gold per metric ton of seawater, ranging from low to high. *But no matter!* There is a lot of water in the seas of the world! The latest tests indicate the probability of ½ to 2 grams of gold per metric ton of seawater, depending upon test-locations and techniques of extraction. This being true, *there is something between 10 and 40 million metric tons of gold out there in the sea*...a quantity that makes our present world stockpile of 80,000 metric tons a mere flyspeck in comparison.

How about you finding and perfecting the necessary process!

Uses For Gold: Old And New

HE DEMANDS FOR GOLD are rising every year...and these demands cannot be met with current rates of newly-mined gold production. Not only is gold still being used by governments to back international financial and commodity exchange agreements, for jewelry, artwork, and for other long-established purposes, it is more and more being demanded by industry and science for needs many of which cannot be done as well — or at all — with other metals.

By 1957, the jewelry, artwork, medical and industrial uses of gold in the U.S. were consuming the entire domestic output of newly-mined gold. By 1965, the U.S. consumption for those same purposes had risen sharply. That year, three times the domestic output of newly-mined gold were required... and science and aerospace uses were greatly adding to the drain on gold reserves. This ravenous trend continues unabated. School class rings alone required 15 metric tons of gold in 1973...more than 33,000 avoir. lbs., about one-third of that year's entire U.S. domestic output of 45 metric tons of newly-mined gold. Here are but a few of the many uses to which gold is now increasingly being put:

Gold's reflectivity — especially in the infra-red end of the spectrum — is making it indispensable...not only in the aerospace program but for today's glass-paneled, air-conditioned buildings. A coating of gold — from 3 to 5 millionths of an inch thick — on the glass permits clear vision outward from within the building...while effectively blocking out most of the solar heat. The savings of electrical energy and lowered air-conditioning equipment costs quickly pay for the gold coating on the glass...which, as a bonus, is also quite beautiful.

Very thin coatings of gold are being used to reflect and thereby confine the fantastic heat generated inside jet engines. This can be mighty important to the fighter plane pilot who sits scant inches above the inferno raging inside the jet engine of his plane! Gold is also now being used as a windshield de-icing method for high-altitude aircraft. A coating of gold only one-fifth of a millionth of an inch thick — interlaced within the laminated windshield glass — does not interfere with the pilot's vision, yet carries sufficient electrical current to heat the glass and thereby prevent icing.

The aerospace program is using thin coatings of gold in many ways. It provides reflectivity where needed, with scant ounces of gold doing the same job normally requiring hundreds of pounds of conventional insulation. It provides corrosion-proof electrical contacts and connections, and it greatly minimizes the weight of interconnecting printed-circuit "wiring" in communications, navigational and computing equipment.

The corrosion-resistance factor of gold is alone proving it to be an economical exterior coating for buildings located in areas suffering from high concentrations of air-borne corrosive pollutants. An example is the Richfield Building, located in Los Angeles. The exterior ceramic was coated with $12,000 worth of gold when the building was erected in 1929. Nearly a half a century later, there is still virtually no evidence of corrosion damage to the gold-protected ceramic exterior. An occasional wash with mild detergent keeps this building looking like a newly-minted coin!

Large quantities of gold are still being used in dental work, although other metals are more and more being used in its stead. This replacement trend is not true of other areas in medicine, however. For example, gold plating is rapidly replacing lead as a lighter, more effective shielding against stray X-rays; it is being used — in the form of a water-soluble salt — in the treatment of arthritis and other ailments. And in the form of colloidal suspensions of radio-active gold, it is more and more being used to fight cancer.

Those who continue to fight against gold simply because of its known stabilizing effects upon world monetary systems are long out of touch with actuality. They are horrified that the price of gold is rising inexorably, in spite of their strenuous efforts to keep gold at 1935 prices...when little else on earth has stayed at those prices. The fact is, so many of today's industrial and scientific needs for gold are so critially important that a price of $1000 per ounce could in many instances be paid...with complete economic justification! Every depleting resource becomes more valuable as needs rise and supplies diminish. Why should gold be different...just to please the high-priests of artificially-contrived currencies and deficit financing?

The Future For Gold

MANKIND IS FORTUNATE that there is such a substance as gold! Admittedly, many excesses have been committed for and because of it...but, is this so different than any other factor of importance in Man's life? *Of course not!* The reality remains that gold has been, is now, and will long remain uniquely capable of fulfilling monetary exchange and value-storage needs better than any other substance now known. There are other reasons, of course, but the five reasons I outline below have for many centuries strongly influenced Man's decisions — and desires — concerning gold:

1) **Universal availability.** Gold is found on every continent; no nation can claim a total monopoly on it. 2) **Relative scarcity.** In spite of its availability, it tends to be scarce and costly to find, mine and refine. This eliminates probable periodic over-supply. 3) **Permanence.** Gold is one of the most stable and permanent substances in the world. Man comes and goes with little to show for his transitory lifespan visit...but gold alone remains sound and beautiful for milleniums. 4) **Density.** Gold is dense, therefore compact. A small fortune can be contained in a single ingot of 995-fine gold only 6 inches wide, 12 inches long and 2 inches thick (about 100 avoir. lbs.). 5) **Divisibility.** Gold is soft, malleable and ductile. It can therefore be easily shaped, re-shaped, and divided up into smaller pieces...or consolidated into larger pieces. This is not true of many other items of value...precious gemstones, for example.

These are the important reasons why men everywhere on earth have for thousands of years considered gold to be the ideal unit of basic value. It has proven to be the one *dependable* medium of exchange, the one *dependable* ally in times of financial need!

Despite the discordant caterwaulings of Keynsian economists (the high-priests of the deficit-financing, planned-inflation cult), gold has not become an anachronism, a "vestigial tail", in the fields of finance and commodity exchange. In spite of their puerile but noisy harangues in favor of GNP, SDR, CRV, and other artificial "fiscal" contrivances, *the fact remains that gold and gold alone has had, does have, and will have the final say in the world of money!*

Theories of economics come and go with the transiency of teenage fads; politicians' promises are of the same substance and dependability as rainbows. But gold...today's gold will still be as true, as useful, as comparatively valuable one thousand years from now as it is today. Can economists and politicians say as much for their theories and promises? And if they say it, can they prove it? *Gold — not theories and promises — has stood the test of time!*

The latest available figures on world gold production indicate a current annual total of approximately 2 million troy pounds of newly-mined gold. Of this amount, the U.S. produces a bit over 6%; Australia, 5%; Russia (a guesstimate only!), 7%; Canada, 15%; So. Africa, 60%...a total of 93%. The balance comes from W. Africa, So. and Central America, India, Japan, New Guinea, Fiji...and in smaller amounts, from Spain, Sweden, Finland and other countries.

But barring the possible discovery and development of rich, new goldfields — and the availability of economically-feasible processes for extracting gold from low-grade colloidal deposits and from seawater — the yearly output of newly-mined gold can only go down...faster and faster, with the passage of time. Why do I say this? Easy! Few new gold producing areas are being developed today; few new mines are being opened...and even fewer old mines are being re-opened. Compounding the problem is a reality that most people tend to forget: *Large or small, there are only so many tons of gold-bearing ores or gold-bearing gravels in each deposit.* Therefore, every existing gold mine in the world today is dying bit by bit...with the extraction of every ton of ore.

For example, it is estimated that the output of the present gold mines in South Africa will begin to diminish quite sharply, probably within 20 years, as the reef deposits begin to play out or get too deep for mining. This will mean the loss of a source that now provides more than half of our needs for newly-mined gold! Gold can only get scarcer, not more plentiful...no matter what the Keynsian eggheads pray for (if they pray!).

No...don't let anyone tell you that gold is going out of style in this new, "modern" age of planned economies! *The placer gold — the flour, bits, pieces and nuggets — that you seek, find and keep today can only grow more and more valuable with the passage of the years!   So, find it and hang onto it!*

HOW TO FIND PLACER GOLD

Where Gold Came From

GOLD ORIGINATED, SO THE GEOLOGISTS SAY, in some as-yet unknown manner, deep within the molten heart of the earth...250 or more million years ago. Somewhat later it came to be deposited — along with other minerals and silica solutions — in the underground cracks and fissures of certain rock formations that are part of the earth's outer crust. The geologists don't even pretend they know for sure how it all happened...but, it did happen, regardless of the theoretical reasons why it couldn't possibly have!

Because of the tremendous pressures that exist deep within the earth, geologists tend to disagree amongst themselves about how cracks, fissures and voids came into existence at those depths. In theory, the very pressures themselves should have prevented such voids from developing. In addition, few geologists can agree on how the voids came to be filled with mineral-bearing silica solutions. They can't even agree on the probable source or sources of the solutions! Guesses they make; ideas they've got; positive opinions and pet theories they expound. Crystal-ball gazers have equally definite opinions and theories and, in truth, are just about as apt to be right. The only thing that is definite about the whole business is that it did happen. Gold came into existence, as did all the other elements...and voids in the basic, magmatic rocks came to be filled with gold-bearing silica solutions. These actualities pose a lot of tough questions for the theory-makers to answer!

We shouldn't judge the geological theory-makers too harshly, however. After all, those events happened many millions of years ago...with no one around to watch and record the precise details. Consequently, geologists can only start out with whatever is known today to be fact and work backward, inductively, from the specific facts of today to generalized conclusions about events that happened long ago. In spite of this severe handicap, geologists have succeeded in producing practical, workable theories that are highly useful to the mining industry. The induced theories most acceptable to the majority of leading geologists indicate the probability of the following sequences and events...a chain of cause and effect that resulted in the formation of primary-deposit gold-bearing ores:

● Certain so-called "basic" granitic rock formations...made up of materials from deep within the earth's molten heart became cracked and fissured. In spite of the tremendous pressures at those depths, the cracks and fissures somehow spread apart in places, creating voids in those faults. These faults extended far down into the earth, into deep zones of newly-formed, extremely hot, mineral-rich basic rock matter.

●   Water solutions containing silica, gold and other minerals ascended up into the fissures and voids. (One theory holds that the hydraulic-pressure effect of the solutions themselves cracked and forced the rocks apart.) Finally, after the passage of sufficient time, the silica and minerals solidified, becoming the mineral-laden rock we now call quartz. Whatever metals were contained in the solutions filling any particular void became part of the make-up of the quartz filling that void. To complicate this neat theory, there are numerous vein structures and ore-bodies to which this sequence apparently does not apply. Fortunately, we can leave these puzzles to others to solve. *You and I do not have to know the answers in order to find placer gold in a mountain stream or desert arroyo...or to work it out with pan, sluice box and dry washers!*

Ignoring the genesis or actual first-creation of gold, then, we can say that it comes to us from two sources. They are:

1) **PRIMARY DEPOSITS:** –
Gold is found in primary (or first) deposits. The mineral/metal bearing rocks are called ores. Such ores have many possible origins. For example, magmatic concentration, sublimation, contact metasomatism, and the hydrothermal processes such as cavity filling and replacement. The gold in the ore will be in two possible forms, (a) native, metallic gold, and (b) gold in compound with tellurium.

Native gold exists in primary ores as individual pieces, however large or small, as inter-connected parts (wire, sheet, moss, leaf, thread, etc.), and -- very rarely – it exists in crystalline form. Crystallization of gold is in the isometric system...usually in dendritic, branching groups. The more common forms taken are cubes, octahedrons and dodecahedrons. Crystalline gold is rare and beautiful enough to be worth far more as specimen pieces than for any other purpose. An exceptionally fine piece – with at least part of the matrix material remaining, the rest carefully etched away with acids – may contain several or more ounces of metallic gold that is quite literally worth its weight in diamonds.

As I have mentioned before, gold readily associates with and joins together with many other metals as alloys...but actually combines only with tellurium. Where gold accompanies the sulfide minerals – arsenopyrite, iron pyrite, chalcopyrite, etc. – and galena, carbonate of bismuth, slate, shale, etc., the gold is usually mixed through the host or matrix material in exceedingly tiny particles and minute scales. Reduction of the mineral mass by crushing and dissolving with acid will usually leave the gold particles clearly visible with a high-power glass. But, when gold is actually combined chemically with tellurium — as calaverite, hessite, sylvanite, krennerite, etc. — not a single speck of gold can be seen, no matter how rich the ore and no matter how powerful the glass. Just a few tons of some gold telluride ores could make you rich as Croesus...but, only with complicated assay procedures would you ever know that gold was present in the rock, and only with complicated refining processes would you ever be able to extract it from that rock!

Gold is obtained from primary deposit ores in which the gold is the principal or only value being sought...and it is also obtained from ores in which the gold is only a bonus by-product. Many copper, lead, zinc and silver mines contain ores with sufficient gold to make its recovery economically feasible. Gold in primary ores may exist in sub-microscopic particles, small flecks and scales, bits and grains, large pieces, and massive chunks. Individual weights of the pieces can range from a millionth of an ounce or so, up to hundreds of pounds.

Primary deposits are mined with standard hard-rock techniques...which are usually expensive, often beset with difficulties, and always requiring geological, engineering and craft skills in abundance. Milling primary deposit ores runs the gamut from the simple *arrastra*, of Spanish days, and usable only with free-milling ores, to the complex equipment and procedures necessary to unlock and recover gold from refractory, compound ores. Except in its most fundamental, free-milling ore form, primary deposit mining and milling is best left to experts and well-financed corporations!

2) SECONDARY DEPOSITS:—

The awesome, mighty forces of Nature have worked ceaselessly — for eons — to liberate gold from ores of primary deposit. Oxidation, acid-reduction, intermittent heating and freezing, earthquakes and volcanoes, faulting, tilting and folding, wind and water erosion, landslides and glacier action...all have worked to free gold from its rock imprisonment and all have done their jobs well. Nature — for her own purposes, whatever they are — has "mined and milled" uncountable millions of tons of gold-bearing hard rocks...and that released gold all went somewhere. Wherever found, such released gold is said to be in secondary deposits. These deposits may be close or far from the ores of original deposit, and they may have gone through countless prior depositings and re-depositings...but they are still called secondary deposits, and the gold is called secondary deposit gold.

When the secondary deposits are located in formerly-loose material that has re-consolidated or metamorphosed for whatever cause — time, temperature, chemical change, etc. — they are called conglomerate secondary deposits, or, simply, conglomerates. Such secondary deposits may occur as veins or reefs, often cemented and fused together into a mass about as hard as the original primary ores, usually deep within the body of the earth. This manner of depositing is typical of the reefs at the Transvaal and Witwatersrand mines of South Africa. More often, they occur as shallower, thicker beds...as at Carlin and Cortez, Nevada.

The conglomerate deposits of South Africa are mined with standard shaft, tunnel and stope hard-rock techniques. Those typical of the Carlin Mine are worked with open-pit methods similar to those used in copper mines. In most cases milling is expensive, requiring reduction of the ore to a fine powder, cyaniding of the resultant gold-laden pulp, zinc-dust precipitation, filtering, and smelting of the final zinc-gold precipitate.

When the secondary deposits are located in loose or relatively loose materials — such as the sands, gravels and rocks of river systems and beaches — the deposits are called placers. *(Incidentally, placer is pronounced "plah-sir"...not "play-sir".)* Gold placers occur in modern-day stream beds and beaches; they occur in gravel benches once part of existing river and beach systems that have been left behind (usually above) by erosion of bedrock or by crustal subsidence or elevation; and they occur in the dead river and beach systems of ancient geological periods...complete with bedrocks, clay, sand and gravel, canyon walls, etc., but completely covered over by volcanic action, crustal faulting, and other changes of similar massive proportions. The techniques of placer mining and placer gold extraction run the gamut from simple panning and pick-and-shovel sluicing to complicated, expensive drift-tunneling, hydraulicking and dredging.

How Gold Got Into The Streams

NDERSTANDING HOW GOLD got into the present-day rivers and streams — especially those of the western high-mountain gold placers — will help you find and recover it more effectively. The probable sequence of events that resulted in secondary deposits of gold undoubtedly varied, region to region. Most geologists seem in agreement, however, that the events and sequences probably occurred much as I outline here...at least in the Sierra Nevadas, Rockies, and other western high-mountain gold producing areas.

Let's begin at the point in geological time when — regardless of how — the gold-bearing vein systems had become fully developed within the rock formations making up the mountain ranges, many of which apparently were very tall...much higher than today. To illustrate, it has been estimated that some of the Sierra Nevadas once towered 25 or more thousand feet above the valley floors. Erosive processes through the ages have actually ground as much as two miles of solid rock off the tops of those still-lofty mountains!

Liberation of the primary deposit gold from the vein structures occurred as a continuous process that lasted for millions of years...as numberless episodes of titanic violence worked at altering the face of the land. Each eon brought its own brands of torment to the mountains: Volcanoes and heat, heaving, uplifting and folding, grinding and crushing, glaciers and freezing. And, at times, as if to wash the whole business away into the sea...flooding torrents of water from seemingly endless rains. Yes, Mother Nature was busy, busy, busy...mining countless billions of tons of ores, and milling out the gold locked within them. On these happenings, there is general agreement amongst geologists. Here is a summary of their conclusions:

● The gold originated, regardless of how, deep within the molten heart of the earth...along with the other minerals.

● The gold came to be distributed throughout the crust of rocks near the surface in veins, as primary deposits.

● Cataclysmic geological changes caused great uplifts and tiltings of the crustal rocks. Mountain ranges raised up and up, high above the surrounding valleys...and the gold-laden vein structures rose up along with them.

● Natural erosive processes began wearing away the rocks...and thus exposed the veins to weather and oxidation. This hastened the liberation of the locked-in gold particles.

●   Torrential floods of rain water washed the liberated gold downhill from the disintegrating vein structures. Even the winds that roared through the mountains helped scatter the released gold far and wide.

●   Downward, ever downward drifted the gold, along with the disintegrated rocks and vein materials. The gold and cubic miles of rock debris eventually found their ways into the ancient river systems. Thus came about the first major secondary gold deposits.

●   There came a new time of great upheavals, of jarring, leveling earthquakes and enormous lava-belching volcanoes. Most of the then-existing river systems soon became completely covered over with incomprehensible tonnages of the materials spewed out by these raging monsters. The gold particles became once again imprisoned...but this time as secondary deposits, buried together with the clays, sands, gravels and boulders of the now-dead river systems that had helped free the gold in the first place.

●   The volcanoes eventually died down, their fires banked by massive plugs of hardened lava. The land became still...and the age of bitter cold arrived. Glaciers formed on the mountain peaks which yet rose high above the lava and ash desolation left behind by the volcanoes. The insistent force of gravity caused the glaciers to begin moving slowly down toward the valleys far below. The constant replenishment of new ice added to the weight of the downward drifting glaciers...and to their power. As they moved downward, they gouged out great furrows, even through solid granite bedrock...as irresistibly as a bulldozer pushing through a child's sand castle on the beach. Where the glaciers cut through the buried, dead-river systems, they released vast quantities of the locked-in secondary deposit gold...which fed into the new, glacier-created channels.

●   Long ages of almost-continuous rainfall again brought gushing floods of water tumbling down from the heights. As each torrent added it power to that of other torrents, the gathered forces became well-nigh irresistible. With the abrasive actions produced by swiftly-moving sands, gravels and boulders, the floods cut deep into the glacier-gouged channel beds...and in many instances formed new channels of their own. The canyons grew ever deeper, ever wider...and the valleys filled with the debris, to form level floors. And all the while the gold particles continued to drift downward. Down hill, down into the sands and gravels, down into the very bedrock itself...in the cracks, crevices and fissures.

Much of the gold in our present-day rivers and streams has obviously undergone countless scatterings, depositings, re-scatterings and re-depositings. But, with each new movement, it always moved downward, drawn inexorably by gravity...downward, until the bits and pieces lodge tightly against solid bedrock or other obstructions it cannot pass through. This downward drift of gold is so uncannily persistent it sometimes seems to me as though it is knowingly seeking out the place of its birth deep within the body of the earth...and that it is trying determinedly, desperately to return to its ancient home!

The time involved during these geological processes (in the Sierra Nevadas, for example) is estimated at about 250-plus million years. A long time, for sure, but only 10 or 15 percent of our earth's estimated total age. Today, the same natural forces continue to work at bringing gold downward from the higher places...but at a far gentler pace. Seekers of placer gold who tend to be most successful are those who remember this downward movement of gold. So they hunt it at the deeper levels of stream beds, bars and benches. And, in their panning, sluicing and dry-washing, they continuously agitate the gold bearing materials being worked, in water or in air, so the gold can move downward to be captured by pan rims, sluice box riffles and similar traps.

Likely Places For It To Be

OLD-TIME PROSPECTORS swear by the statement, *"Gold is where you find it!"* And, in truth, it has been found in some of the strangest places. But, it is a safe bet that far more gold has been found as the result of gold-savvy, common sense, hard work, and that strange sixth-sense we call "intuition" than as the result of accidental discoveries and the smiles of Lady Luck. It is true, of course, that the amounts of gold deposited in any given area — or whether any at all was deposited — seem to be the result of Fate's often whimsical caprices. But, what happens to gold after it has gotten into the rivers and streams happens as the direct results of well-known natural forces. Its movements in those waterways can, therefore, be predicted with reasonable accuracy.

To be successful at finding gold, you must first learn how those natural forces act upon gold. This knowledge and understanding can be yours simply for the learning and memorizing of the following facts about gold and what happens when it is forcibly agitated and moved about in a sand-gravel-water mixture. The first fact is so important that I have repeated it many times throughout the book:

SIX IMPORTANT "GOLD FACTS"

1) **Gold is heavy.** Therefore, the force of gravity causes it to work its way downward, ever downward: a) downhill; b) downstream; c) down into the sands and gravels; d) down into bedrock cracks and crevices; e) down into soft bedrocks; f) down into the bottoms of pans and sluice boxes.

2) **Gold is assisted in its downward movement by agitation.** Water, wind, earth-tremors and mechanical movement provide or aid the agitation.

3) **Gold tends to take the shortest possible route for its travels,** both downward and downstream. Gravity pulls it downward; water power pulls it downstream. Therefore, gold tends to hug the inside, short bank of curves and bends in the streams.

4) **Gold tends to concentrate at any point where obstructions hinder or stop its progress.** Boulders, sills, dikes and other natural barriers, sluice box riffles, and the up-turned rims of gold pans all work for this reason.

5) **Gold tends to concentrate at any point where the water-flow slows down.** Slack water lacks the power necessary to drag gold on downstream.

6)   Gold tends to do the five things listed above in proportion to the weight and shape of the individual pieces. In other words: a) the heavier the pieces, the more closely the facts are followed; b) the rounder and denser the pieces, the more the facts are followed; c) the lighter the pieces, the less the facts are followed; d) the flatter or thinner the pieces, the less the facts are followed.

Since Gold Facts No. 1 and No. 2 are practically self-explanatory, let's start out with an examination of No. 3. *Keep in mind that gold is heavy...*and keep in mind also that *gold is much less pushed downstream by the water than it is dragged along by the power of the water.* Because of this "dragged downstream" action, the effect of centrifugal force plays but a minor part in the path taken by all but the lightest, flattest pieces. Remember, *gold always tends to take the shortest possible route as it follows a stream's meanderings.* It will generally be found in the greatest concentrations along the short or inside banks of the curves and bends. This is especially true of the heavier, denser pieces. The flour and very light pieces are tossed about more readily by the water and often wind up on the far, outside arcs of the curves.

It will help you understand this "dragged downstream" effect if you will take a moment and visualize the following scene in your mind's eye. To start...see a section of a mountain stream, long enough to include some bends and turns. Next...see a length of rope that is laid out along the bottom of the stream bed and extending the whole length of your imaginary stream. See a heavy weight, tied onto the upstream end of the rope. Now then, see yourself at the downstream end...beginning to pull rope and weight toward yourself.

The rope tightens up all the way back to the weighted end and begins to move downstream, along the stream bed. As it moves, the rope quickly slides into positions that put it into the shortest possible pathway...not only around the bends but in the straight-aways between bends. The individual fibers of the rope move along downstream, passing by each given spot in the stream bed. But, as you continue to pull the rope toward you, the body of the rope itself will stay in about the same position or track along the stream bed. This shortest pathway taken by the rope is the one most likely to be taken by the gold during its downstream movement. And the many possible exceptions notwithstanding, extensive prospecting by beginners that is too far off of this line will be apt to prove a waste of time and effort.

While the above visualization is an admitted over-simplification, it does serve to illustrate how a heavy object, being *dragged* downstream, does not swing out wide on the curves...as it would if being pushed by the water.

Remember, *the out-swinging effect of centrifugal force is but a small factor in the downstream drifting of gold.* You must also remember that individual stream conditions dictate the pathway the gold actually will take...and every stream is somewhat different: Water volume and velocity, large boulders, rock slides, eddies and whirlpools, bedrock sills and dikes that project out into or up into the stream, stream fall or rate of descent, the average size and shape of the gold particles, the percentages of clay, sand and gravel in the stream bed, etc.

Figuring out the probable line of movement in any particular stream is never exactly like baking a batch of ready-mix biscuits; there is more to it. But this very difficulty probably accounts in large part for the thrill...when you do succeed!

Next, let's go to Gold Fact No. 4: This one is also easy to understand because it is obvious that *gold can't go where it is a physical impossibility for it to go!* For similar cause...if you walk up against a stone wall, you stop; so it is with gold: When it gets to a "stone wall" obstruction it can't go under, around or over...it stops. This is equally true whether the obstruction is a rock ledge, sill or dike, a boulder, a raise or "horse" in the bedrock, a riffle in a sluice box, or the upturned rim of your gold pan. Remember Gold Fact No. 1: *Gold is heavy.* It takes power to lift gold up and over obstructions. The heavier the piece of gold...the more power necessary to get the job done.

It requires obstructions of different kinds to stop and to hold the various sizes and shapes of gold particles. A riffle made by nailing a 1" by 1" cleat across the bottom of a sluice-box will stop heavy nuggets and most of the coarse gold. The "fines" (flour and tiny, flaky particles) will usually wash right up and over such a cleat. This is the reason why the roughest sort of panning techniques are usually good enough to save nuggets and small, dense pieces; it is also the main reason why considerable care is required to save the fines. *And not only care, but knowledge!*

To save the fines in sluice boxes, miners generally place a special type of corduroy cloth -- or carpeting, burlap, etc., -- under iron screens or gratings in their sluice boxes. The same technique is often used when panning where most of the pay is in fines. In more extreme situations, it is even necessary to add mercury to the sluice boxes and pans. Incidentally, the mosses that grow on the rocks of many mountain streams make ideal fine-gold catchers. In fact, in streams where a large percentage of the gold is in fines, a good part of your pay can come from washing out these mosses. If you hear someone talking about "moss-mining", this is what they mean.

E.S. LeGaye: 1966

Placer gold from the Sandella Mine. This gold runs from 925 to 940 fine, and because of its deep, rich color and rugged "nugget" appearance, it is highly prized by collectors. When sold as specimens, such gold often brought as much as $150 per ounce even when the official price was still $35. It is obviously much more valuable now! Believe it, by the time you find your gold, mine it, fight off the eager-beavers from the Bureau of Land Management, Forest Service, Fish and Game Commission, ad nauseum—and at the same time, protect yourself against vandals and sluice box robbers—it is worth every dime you can get!

Dan E. LeGaye: 1969

Adele M. Stagner, the writer's mother, panning out a top-of-the-string sluice box cleanup at her Sandella Mine, located high in the Sierra Nevadas, about 20 air-miles east of Forest-hill, California. Isolated? Yes! The last few miles of "road" require 4-wheel-drive. 80-plus years old now, Mother is a 3rd generation gold miner with much experience at finding and recovering placer gold in paying quantities. Gold has long been in our family "blood"!

E.S. LeGaye: 1966

A.M. Stagner, using a small, specially-riffled sluice to work main sluice box concentrates. Such a sluice makes easier the tedious job of separating the gold fines from large amounts of black sand. Limited water flow, nearly-level box and much patience are required!

Gold Fact No. 5 is also simple to understand, but at the same time, important to prospectors. *The forces generated by water moving downstream furnishes the power that moves the gold.* It is the dynamic energy of the flowing water that lifts gold up over obstructions and around obstacles: *The lighter the piece of gold, or the stronger the flow, the easier it is for the water to keep the gold moving downstream.* Whenever the stream bed widens out, the water slows down and loses some of its force: *The less force, the less power. The less power, the less gold moved.* Whenever the total volume of water in the stream diminishes, the dropout of gold along the stream bed will tend to be uniform. Wherever the reductions of water-force are due to localized widenings of stream beds, the gold will tend to concentrate just below each widening. Because the sands and gravels being carried along by the water also tend to drop out at such points, gold-bearing gravel bars build up there.

Finally, we come to Gold Fact No. 6, which is almost self-explanatory. It stands to reason that *the heavier the piece of gold, the more power required to move it and keep it moving.* A tiny fleck, perhaps flattened by being smashed between two rocks, will not likely follow the same path downstream taken by a half-ounce nugget. The tiny piece is much more apt to be tossed from side to side by the water pressures exerted on its flattened surfaces. Being light as well, such bits of gold will tend to remain in motion long after the flow has slowed down enough to drop out the heavier, rounder pieces.

SOME MISCELLANEOUS FACTS

Since I have used the term, *"gold-bearing gravel bar,"* I can almost see your eyes light up, and I can almost hear you say, *"Aha! Now we're getting someplace! Lots of sand and gravel in one spot...with all that good ol' gold mixed all in it. Now, that's for me!"* So, before you dash off for a life of fame and wealth as a sand-and-gravel bar gold panner, let's stop a moment right here and analyze the mathematics involved. Let's do what might best be called a "feasibility evaluation".

● The most skilled of professionals — working the very easiest sort of sand and gravel deposits — can handle no more than one cubic yard of material a day with a gold pan.

● Gravel that carries from 5 to 10 dollars in gold per cubic yard is considered very good for working with a sluice box...with an average daily production of 3 to 10 yards per man. *(And believe me, that's a lot of work. I know, because I've done it!)*

● Working with a pan, a yard of gravel — even at 10 dollars per cubic yard — means a day's pay of less than 10 dollars...which is no princely sum for digging out and panning a ton and a half of sand and gravel!

● *This is why I now say, "pans are for crevices, pot-holes and bedrock scrapings!"* You probably won't believe me until you try for yourself.

Your best chance for successful panning is to hunt for the "hot spots" where gold has had the chance to accumulate in Nature's own "sluice box" systems. By doing this, you will save yourself many a disappointment and backache. Try always to work mainly the material that lies along the bedrock of natural concentration points. I cannot stress too strongly that for the man depending on a gold pan alone for pay, the best returns generally come from working the material on and in bedrock...in the cracks, crevices, soft-spots and small, rough-walled pot-holes.

This "bedrock mining" has its own techniques, none of which are really complicated...but each with its reason for being and relative importance, its own priority. For a starter — after finding a place worth working — you either pick a spot that is already somewhat free of sand and and gravel overburden... or, you shovel away the overburden until you get to within an inch or so of bedrock. *(I know, I know! There are such things as false bedrocks that also serve to hold gold, and I know that a suddenly-diminishing stream flow can leave even coarse gold high up in paystreaks...well above bedrock. I also know that — at least in the California placers — the Chinese miners who followed the 49'ers gleaned every speck of gold off of the bedrocks they worked! But, what I say above holds true in the average. And only experience provides the know-how of when to deviate far afield from the averages!)*

Next, if you start your work on the downstream end and on the inside bank of a bend in the stream and start working upstream, you're stacking the odds of success in your favor. And when you have reached the bedrock, if you find it full of cracks, criss-crossed with small veins of decomposed quartz, and/or soft enough to sink your pick into it easily, start getting excited. This is good prospecting ground for the man with a pan...and good ground is where you have the best chance to find the good pay!

Any bedrock crack big enough for water to get into is also big enough for gold to get into. I have often been amazed at the amount of flour gold that can be taken from one tiny, almost hair-line crack. Such bedrock cracks and fissures are often of such a nature that you can lever the pieces apart with your pry-bar...which you must of course do in order to get the gold.

You will sometimes find bedrock that is soft enough to drive the point of a pick into for an inch or two...and such bedrock will catch and hold gold. During the mid-1930's, I saw a number of California placers where the miners moved off hundreds of yards of low-pay overburden, in order to pick down into and get such soft bedrock into their sluice boxes...and make, incidentally, a good profit on the entire undertaking. This kind of project is beyond the capability of the weekend or vacation panner, of course, but the principle holds true, regardless. *You will find the bulk of your gold down low...near bedrock, on bedrock and in bedrock.* But getting down to bedrock is usually hard work...which is why gold mining is not for the faint hearted or weak. *Panning gold for fun is one thing; mining gold for a living is another!*

Some of the best crevices for catching gold were caused by the oxidation and decomposition of small quartz veins that crisscross the bedrock. While the rough surfaces of such cracks are hard to clean — and often do not break apart readily — they do catch gold! The big fault-lines that you find above the water level are also good places. Generally, you will do well to avoid trying to work below the level of water, as it takes gold-savvy and experience to recover gold from under water successfully and consistently. Experienced prospectors working small streams often make use of a device called a "gold sniffer" for recovering gold from under water. These are small, hand-held suction devices which will pick up much of the gold from accessible, underwater bedrock cracks and crevices.

You will occasionally run across small pot-holes in the bedrock — a few inches to a foot or more in diameter and as deep — that also resulted from decomposition of quartz. As long as the inside surfaces are rough, they are worth cleaning out. But, the small, glass-smooth pot-holes that you generally find are almost always a disappointment. About all they are apt to contain is a fleck or two of flour, some black sand, pyrites, etc. You can easily lose up to half an hour of your time cleaning out and panning any one of them.

Many times, beginners get all excited and worked up about finding big pot holes in the bedrock — often five feet or more in diameter and as deep — and generally about in the center of nearly-dry streams. As a matter of fact, when you stand on the bank and look at one, that big hole in the bedrock can give you a funny sort of feeling. It really does seem that all the gold that ever came down the stream just had to fall into it!

But, as gold catchers, these big babies are nearly all phonies! Ninety-nine times out of a hundred it is a complete waste of time even to poke a stick into them, much less to clean them out. A little serious thought on the subject will show you why spending your time cleaning them out would eventually make you poor as a church-mouse. Take a moment; visualize in your mind's eye what goes on in their innards during periods of high water. Water foaming in and out, swirling and churning; rocks crashing and thumping, grinding and crushing everything they hit, including the very walls of the pot-holes themselves; sand and gravel...scouring and scraping like a water-borne sand blaster. If I were you, I'd not get too excited over the possibility of getting rich by working the contents of these nature-made "ball mills"! About all they are good for (?) is to convert nuggets into flour gold.

As you prospect along any stream bed known to carry gold, be particularly alert for evidences of ground that has never been worked. Such spots will usually be small...just little patches of ground overlooked by previous prospectors and miners. They are not hard to recognize, once you know what to look for; usually cemented sand and gravel, possibly under very old trees along the stream. More on cemented gravel is explained later.

Many good areas can still be found in the high bedrock areas — benches, they are usually called — that were formed many years ago...and left high and dry by gradual, erosion-caused lowering of the stream beds. Such benches are common in the streams of the West and are all worth prospecting. But, obviously, you cannot mine off such a bench with just your pan!

There are a number of things — visible signs — that experienced prospectors and miners look for as indicators of the presence or possible presence of gold. Naturally, these indicators can vary widely from area to area and stream to stream. But, the following are high up on any list of good signs. When you run into them, be on the lookout for gold!

● **Black Sand:—** This is a group of minerals, rather than a single one. All are quite heavy in relationship with ordinary sands and gravels...though much lighter than gold. The minerals in this group include: Hematite and magnetite, the platinum family of minerals, chromite, rutile and ilmenite, monazite, cassiterite, diamond, garnet and zircon. Not all occur in every black sand deposit. These minerals range in color from red to black, although most appear black when wet...especially in your gold pan.

The presence of black sand — even in large quantities — is not of itself a proof of gold. But most of the richer gold placers also carry black sand...often in large amounts. When you find black sand, therefore, look sharply; placer gold could be nearby. Black sand itself can be valuable, especially when heavily charged with the titanium minerals, rutile and ilmenite...and it often contains exceedingly fine flour and colloidal gold in surprising quantity. But, for most weekend panners and vacation prospectors, black sand tends to be more a nuisance than an asset...even if it is a good indicator for locating gold.

The iron oxides, hematite and magnetite, are the black sands you will encounter most. Hematite is red to dark red, 70% iron, non-magnetic. Magnetite is dark red to black, 75% iron, magnetic (it is attracted to a magnet). Hematite is fairly easy to slough off out of your pan, but large quantities of magnetite will test your panning skill and make you earn your fine gold! Magnetite also clogs the riffles of a sluice box so tightly that, unless it is occasionally cleaned out, all the fine gold and much of the heavier gold will pass right over the riffles...and out the end of the box. *And that's bad!*

But black sand — especially hematite and magnetite — have another feature, this one more redeeming. Their high mineralization affects most electronic metal detectors...which makes possible the use of these instruments for the locating of black sand concentrations and — hopefully — placer gold deposits.

● **Water-Worn Rocks:—** Well-rounded gravel and boulders indicate a lot of wear...which in turn indicates a probable origin in the ancient river channels. The round, white cobbles of quartz found in parts of California's Mother Lode country are a particularly good sign; they are mostly from one extremely prolific gold-producing era...the *Eoscene.* The hydraulically-mined placers of the Deadwood - Michigan Bluff areas of Placer County were rich not only in gold but in these rounded white quartz cobbles. There are literally millions of them remaining in the old tailings piles of these mines!

If the rocks in a stream are mostly sharp and angular, they probably are of a more local origin and haven't traveled far. In California's Sierra Nevadas, for example, such rocks indicate streams that are not likely to contain gold from any of the ancient river channel systems which provided most of the gold found in the richer placers. Such sharp, angular rocks do not eliminate the possibility of good gold deposits, however. They are, by themselves, merely an indication of limited travel. One of New Mexico's richest placer fields, the Wicks Gulch — Gold Dust — Ready Pay Canyon area of Sierra County, originated from the erosion of a thousand or more feet in heighth off the top of Animas Peak, the site of the primary source veins. Probably none of the gold in this field has traveled more than 10 miles, but even in that short distance, most of the accompanying rocks became quite smoothed and rounded.

● **Cemented Gravel:—** This is gravel (usually water-worn) that is cemented together with clay. In the Sierra Nevadas, this clay is usually either a slate blue or rusty red. The gold bearing, cemented gravels of Central New Mexico tend to be bonded by a pinkish clay. And I have seen good paying gravels in Arizona, Nevada and Southern California in which the clays ranged from dirty white to yellow and to gray. In many of these cemented gravels, the bond is so strong that you actually have to hammer the chunks to break them up. Not as hard as rock or concrete, but too hard to dissolve in a pan or sluice box. If you're not in a hurry you can let the chunks weather in the open for a year or so. That usually — but not always — does the trick. If the deposit is large enough and rich enough, a ball mill is the best answer...but that's another sort of project!

You should always be watchful for pockets of this material in streams known to have been good producers of placer gold in the past...especially when prospecting in the Sierra Nevadas. The reason is simple: This cemented gravel has been in that one spot for tens of thousands of years and is exactly as Nature left it. Whatever gold was in or under such gravel is still there. Most good "lucky finds" made by panners during the last 75 or so years have come from this type of gravel.

Now, a few words about "fool's-gold", the name commonly given to certain micas and pyrites (biotite mica and iron sulfide, for example, both of which are yellowish minerals). There will be but little likelihood of your being "fooled" by such minerals if you will but do a bit of practical testing. The mica particles are quite light, and are easily split apart or broken to pieces with the point of a sharp knife; all pyrites are much lighter than gold, with a typical sp. gr. of 5, and are easily crushed into a brownish powder in your pan. An old miners's adage says, *"If you have something that you're not sure is gold, it probably isn't gold!"* There are many exceptions, of course; manganese and iron stained gold, mercury-coated gold, etc. But, for beginning prospectors, the adage is true enough for most practical purposes. The "natural state" placer gold that you will be finding in your pan won't keep you in doubt. For the greater part, when you see a piece of real gold in your pan, you'll know that it is gold!

Using Metal Detectors To Locate Placers

ELECTRONIC METAL DETECTORS are a recent addition to the prospectors' tool-kits. They really are capable of helping locate placer gold...but generally only in certain locations and under the right circumstances. The "how-it-works" is easy to understand, as there are only a few basic facts involved. The "how-to-do-it" is a bit more difficult to grasp...as it requires not only understanding of the basics, but adequate experience with a suitable detector and mastery of search techniques.

HOW IT WORKS:—

Even good detectors can only locate gold nuggets when they are large enough. The smaller the nugget, the smaller the required detector search head ...and the less distance the nugget will be detectable. Most manufacturers make small-diameter sensors — from 1" to 3" — which are usually called nugget probes. But, even such special-purpose probes must be brought quite close to a nugget in order to detect it...especially one lying buried in the electromagnetically complex ground that is characteristic of most stream beds in mineralized areas. The large nugget that lies open, on bedrock swept relatively clear of sand and gravel, is of course a findable target. The truth is, this is a rare event these days. Nuggets tend to be frustratingly small...and worse, they are usually buried deep down in the sands and gravels. Consequently, placer gold is generally a poor target, just about beyond the field-practical detection capabilities of most detectors...even good ones.

Not just any old box that buzzes will do. It must be a detector designed and built for such severe service. To be suitable for prospecting, your instrument must have the following qualities: 1) **Waterproof search head**, etc.; up to the control housing. 2) **Frequency-stable (drift resistant) operation**; capable of functioning steadily even when the search head is immersed in ice cold water. 3) **Sensitive, high-gain circuitry**; capable of responding even to very slight changes of matrix and target permeability and conductivity. And, 4) **Rugged design and construction**; tough enough to stand both impact and thermal shocks, tight enough to resist dust and moisture. In short, your detector must work as needed, where needed, when needed. Nothing else is good enough. Many makes or models of detectors that are adequate for park and school yard coinshooting simply cannot cut the mustard when used for prospecting. So...when buying an instrument for this work, be sure to let your dealer — or the manufacturer — know exactly what you have in mind. It could save you time, money, disappointment and aggravation.

HOW TO DO IT:—

● Rather than seek gold itself, then, today's smart prospector uses his detector to locate deposits of magnetic black sand. Why? *Easy!* This material accompanies placer gold in most districts, often in large, easily detectable amounts. And, since these black sands are much heavier than common sand and gravel, they tend to accumulate in precisely the same locations where placer gold accumulates. So...when you locate a sizable concentration of black sand, yell, *"Eureka!"* You have also located (maybe!) a concentration of gold.

Personally, I prefer a beat frequency (BFO) detector for prospecting. Some makes of transmitter receiver (more correctly, induction balance) detectors can also be used, however...but, in my opinion, with reduced efficiency. My own choice of detector for this hard, demanding work is a Garrett BFO Master Hunter...but there are other manufacturers who also make suitable detectors. Regardless of whose instrument you choose, *try before you buy!*

● When you are on site, tune your (BFO) detector to the "mineral" mode setting, so that concentrations of black sand will cause a rising audio tone. Search slowly. listening carefully for changes that indicate minerals in quantity. Keep the loop as close to the ground as possible. If erratic mineralization causes you much difficulty, you can sometimes reduce the trouble by raising the loop just a bit...and still detect black sand concentrations. Obviously, not all indications are going to come from black sand...and not all black sand concentrations are going to carry gold in paying quantities. *The only way to know is to dig and pan!*

The most efficient and profitable use of your detector when prospecting comes not from searching for nuggets that lie under water, nor from searching dry land benches. It comes, instead, from working running streams in advance of a high-quality suction dredge! Where you find gobs of black sand, you stick the nozzle of the dredge...possibly to find gobs of gold. Most people are unaware of the really large amounts of gold being recovered nowadays by experienced operators who use these techniques and first-class equipment...in places where gold is yet to be found in abundance. *And there are such places!*

W.L. Baugh: 1970

Ray V. Erdman, now deceased, demonstrating the well-nigh forgotten art of dry panning flour gold...at his mine near the old ghost town of Gold Dust, N.M. Dry panning requires a great deal of practice to save even the coarser bits of gold. To save the fines, you must completely master this simple-appearing but incredibly-difficult art. Muscles help too!

E.S. LeGaye: 1962

Everybody is fascinated by the possibility of seeing gold in a partially-worked pan of material creviced from bedrock of proven richness! Wayne Fieldhouse, Bonnie and Dan LeGaye, and A.M. Stagner...at the confluence of Big and Little Secret Canyons, just down stream from the long-abandoned Greek Mine—of reputed great richness and dark mysteries.

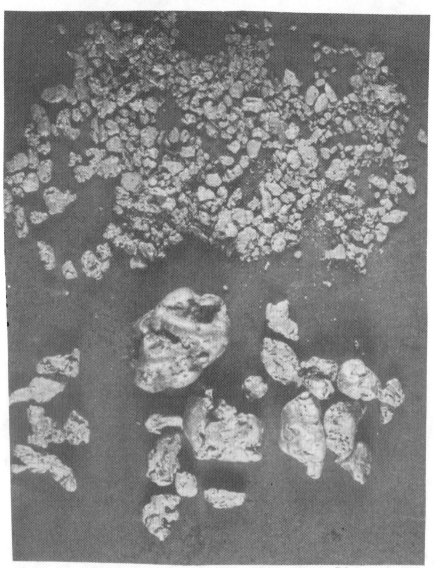

E.S. LeGaye: 1966

A closer look at some of the gold from Glenn Edghill's undergound placer, the East Branch Mine (once known as the Ford Mine). Glenn is another of the rapidly-vanishing breed, men with the accumulation of wisdom we call "gold-savvy"...experience-proven knowledge gathered during a lifetime of seeking, finding and recovering gold, men whose retirement leaves America infinitely poorer for the loss. Those who have never mined gold professionally can have no idea at all of the incredible labors (and courage!) of such men as Glenn. Day after day they go—often alone—into pitch-black tunnels and shafts deep inside remote mountains...to drill, blast, dig, timber, and cart out ore and waste. Often with little more to sustain them than independence, resourcefulness and faith, they carry on...even during the bad times that cause men of weaker fibers to hesitate or quit the fight. Such strengths are truly a part of our national assets, yet—shamefully—these are the men whom our bureaucratic hirelings are being paid to drive off the publicly-owned lands. And—even more shamefully!—there are many people in the America of today who don't even care.

THE NECESSARY EQUIPMENT

The Gold Pan

YOUR GOLD PAN is the "star" performer of your equipment. Just about everything else used is either to help you get the gold into the pan, or to get it out and into safe-keeping. Actually, almost any open-top container or pan a foot or so in diameter and with an upturned edge or rim at least a couple of inches high can be used as a gold pan...frying pans and wash basins, for example. But, the standard miner's gold pan came about as the result of many years's of trial and error development. It is designed to simplify working off the worthless material while, at the same time, saving all or most of the gold put into it...and for ease of handling, ruggedness, and long-lasting dependability.

Gold pans come in various sizes, from about 8 inches to as much as 18 inches in diameter. Most have rims that slope at about 45 degrees, and are about 2 to 3 inches deep. Some are perfectly smooth, others have riffle-like indentations stamped or molded into them...to help save fine gold. Even better for this purpose are pans made with screen and cloth devices attached to the pan bottoms. They hang onto fine gold that all but the most expert panner would probably lose. It is easy to convert a standard pan to this type.

Most gold panners prefer the larger pans because small pans hold perhaps half as much material...yet require nearly as much time and effort to work off that material. In the final analysis, the "best" pan for you is the one that will do your job most efficiently and that you feel most comfortable using.

You must remove every trace of oil and grease from your pan before putting it to use...especially if there is much fine gold in the ground you will be working. This is easy to do with a strong detergent, and — with steel pans — it is best done with heat. Properly done, heat not only cleans the pan, it leaves it a beautiful dark blue color that makes even the little particles of gold show up better. Here is how this is done: Heat your steel pan in the coals of a wood fire until it is beginning to turn a dull red...then drop it into cold water. The pan will change to a dark

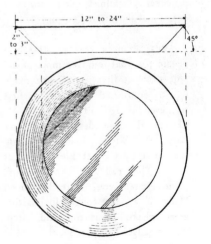

STANDARD MINER'S GOLD-PAN

blue color as it cools and, of course, every speck of oil or grease is gone. If the blue isn't dark enough, or if it is not uniform, simply re-heat and try again. The only way you can hurt your pan by doing this would be to greatly overheat it...which isn't likely, using a wood fire.

A good steel pan will take an awful lot of abuse and still do a good job for you for a long time...many years, in fact. But there is a practical limit, so try to take care of your pan...and it will take care of you. Don't fill your pan full of dents and dings by driving tent stakes with it; don't leave water and black sand in it for long periods of time...as the resultant rust damage is mean to remove. Remember, *a smooth, clean, properly-blued steel gold pan is a joy to use and a pleasure to behold!*

There is little that man has developed during past years that someone isn't now duplicating in plastic. (Not necessarily cheaper, seldom better or even as good.) Feeling as I do about plastic imitations, when I first saw a plastic gold pan some years ago, the only repeatable part of what I thought and said was, *"Ecccch!"* What could you do with one except take care of it like a baby and pan gold with it until it wore out... which I knew wouldn't take long, due to the soft plastics used. (When I was prospecting — 'way back when — I used my trusty old steel pan for many tasks other than panning: making coffee, cooking bacon and pancakes, heating water for my occasional shaves, and so on.)

But, about a year ago, I saw a plastic pan that removed most of my objections at first glance, and made me a confirmed booster at first try...even if I can't cook with it! This is the pan designed by Roy Lagal, of Lewiston, Idaho, and manufactured by Garrett Electronics, of Dallas. They call it a "Gravity-Trap" ...and, I tell you, it really works. Made of a super-tough, long-lasting green plastic, it is the gold catching'est gadget I've ever seen!

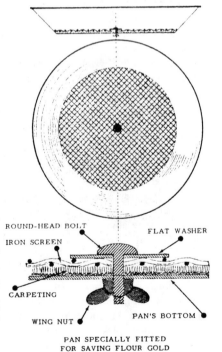

ROUND-HEAD BOLT

IRON SCREEN

FLAT WASHER

CARPETING

WING NUT

PAN'S BOTTOM

PAN SPECIALLY FITTED
FOR SAVING FLOUR GOLD

Brushes, Tweezers, Crevicing-Tools

SEVERAL SMALL BRUSHES are an absolute must. One can be a whisk-broom, the other a paint brush that is from one to two inches wide. The inexpensive nylon brushes sold in most paint stores will do quite nicely. They last a long time and don't cost much. Use these brushes for your final clean-up of exposed bedrock areas. This brushing-up of bedrock is a vitally-important part of your panning work. It really doesn't make sense to dig off a ton or so of sand and gravel...and then leave a lot of the gold lying on the bedrock because you failed to brush it up! In many places, at least half your pay will be in the dried silt and sand that you brush up off of bedrock and out of the bedrock fissures.

A PAIR OF TWEEZERS may not be an absolute necessity, but they sure do help you get your bits and pieces of gold out of the pan and into the bottle. Any good, pointed pair will do; either chrome plated or stainless steel is best.

CREVICING TOOLS are used for gouging, digging, scraping and prying. Most are home-made, "plain-janes," made from all sorts of odds and ends: old screwdrivers, files, broken kitchen knives, coat hangers, small crow-bars, etc. And then some are really fancy...made by machinists or blacksmiths, complete with hardwood handles, brass bindings, knurlings and case-hardened scraping edges. But they all do exactly the same job: They get the gold up out of pot-holes, cracks and crevices. Without crevicing tools, you might as well leave your gold-pan at home...for all the good that you will be apt to do with it. For your first trip out, you can use an old file, with the tang-end bent over about 90 degrees, or an old screwdriver with the shank bent, a small pry-bar, and a steel knife. Actual work in the bedrock of the stream you're panning will show exactly what you need in just a few hours.

Don't stint yourself on quality, sturdiness, and lightness when gathering up the equipment you will use in your prospecting and panning! You not only want your tools to do their job with the least possible amount of effort on your part...you want them to last. A worn-out brush or a broken pry-bar can mean the difference between getting gold or going home with an empty bottle.

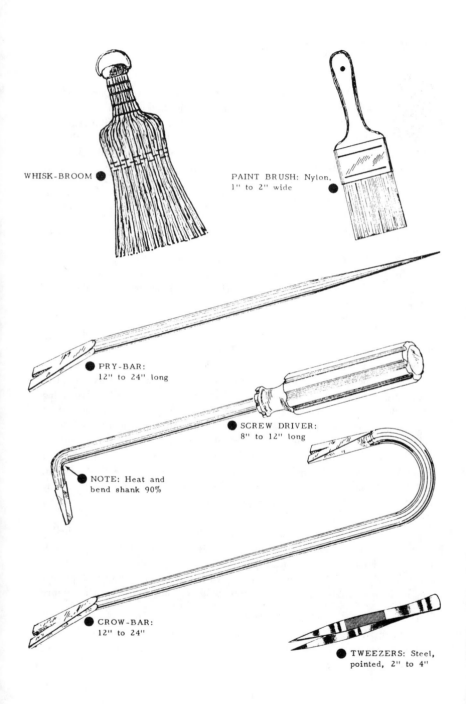

WHISK-BROOM ●

PAINT BRUSH: Nylon,
1" to 2" wide ●

● PRY-BAR:
12" to 24" long

● SCREW DRIVER:
8" to 12" long

● NOTE: Heat and
bend shank 90%

● CROW-BAR:
12" to 24"

● TWEEZERS: Steel,
pointed, 2" to 4"

SHORT-HANDLED SHOVELS weigh less and are easier to pack along with the rest of your prospecting gear. As long as you are pot-holing and crevicing, the short-handled shovel is easily your best bet. Another advantage is the fact that you are much less likely to break the handle by using your shovel as a pry-bar! Such an accident is no laughing matter, when you are 'way out in the boondocks...and lose your main digging tool.

LONG-HANDLED SHOVELS are best, however, if you need to move any amount of yardage. They are faster and easier on your back. Regardless of your good intentions to the contrary, you will doubtless be using your shovel to pry up rocks and roots...so get a good one; well-reinforced and sturdy.

G.I. SHOVELS of the folding type are all right if you are trying to pack as light as possible. They don't move much dirt — for the effort and back-aches involved — but, with patience and much hard work, they will do an acceptable job.

Whichever shovel you do get, be sure that it has a rounded point! Square-point shovels are a lost cause for the prospector...being well-nigh impossible to use in the sands and gravels of the average stream bed.

STEEL TEASPOONS and tablespoons are a necessity. A lot of the best pot-holes and crevices are far too small to get your shovel into. If you don't want to use your fingers for cleaning out such places (and they sure wouldn't last long!), carry several spoons with you. Like the rest of your equipment, they should be sturdily made. The cheaper, dime-store variety is usually too light to do the job. Go to a hardware store and get a good one...because you will find that a really strong teaspoon and tablespoon will double your take when you are working rough bedrock. Actually, they are the handiest little "shovels" you ever saw!

STANDARD MINER'S PICKS are your best bet for prospecting and pan-ning work. They are light and strong, and they will stand up under a lot of hard work. Railroad picks, clay picks and mattocks are all much too heavy for the prospector to try packing around in the field. Railroad picks are exceptionally strong and are good for prying rocks up out of clay and roots... but they weigh too much for the prospector to pack along with everything else that he has to carry.

GEOLOGIST'S PICKS, with one of the points squared off like a hammer, are handy to have along. You will undoubtedly find enough use of one to justify carrying it with you.

A SINGLE-BITTED AXE is a must. If you plan to prospect within the National Forest areas, you must carry an axe as well as a shovel. Regulations or not, however, an axe provides insurance against the dangers of fallen trees and other such road blockages...all common enough occurrences in the high mountain country. You can cut firewood with a hatchet...but it's an awfully t·ugh job to use a little, scout-type hatchet to cut through a two-foot spruce log in the middle of a stormy, rain-lashed night. So, take an axe! *Don't buy a double bitted axe;* they are for professional woodsmen and are dangerous for amateurs to use. *Keep your axe sharp;* it is the dull axe that causes the serious accidents.

MECHANICAL CONTRIVANCES of various kinds can be included with the equipment taken along on your prospecting trips...all of which will just be in your way and add unnecessary weight if you don't need or use them. But...if you do happen to need one or all, you'll not only be thankful you took them, you'll undoubtedly brag (just a little, at least!) about your far-sighted preparedness. Such contrivances include:

A small gasoline-powered chain saw; a lever-operated come-along and at least 50 feet of good chain; a small gasoline-powered centrifugal pump, with strainer protected suction hose and perhaps 50 feet of canvas discharge hose; etc., etc. There can be no "total" list, since the possible requirements vary widely from location to location and condition to condition. The chain saw will be many times faster than the axe at cutting away deadfalls blocking the road; the come-along can be used for moving heavy objects out of your way, and for freeing your stuck vehicle. (If you've never been in such a predicament — 50 or 100 miles from the nearest help — you haven't the foggiest idea of how welcome a sight a good come-along and piece of chain can really be!); the pump can provide water for ground sluicing, for regular sluice boxes located away from the stream, and for panning. (It's far easier to move water to the average site than to move material to the water!)

It is well to remember that almost every one of these (and other) tools and gadgets necessary or useful to prospecting, gold recovery, transportation, and daily existence in the out-of-doors is potentially hazardous...not of itself, necessarily, but in careless or ignorant use. Such use can injure, often seriously. It can also kill.

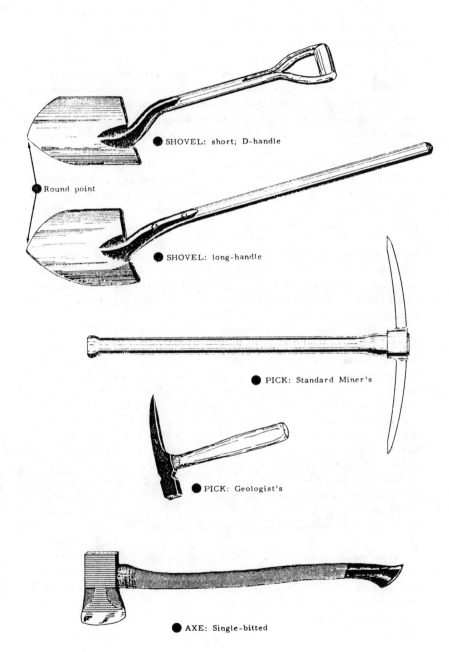

SHOVEL: short; D-handle

Round point

SHOVEL: long-handle

PICK: Standard Miner's

PICK: Geologist's

AXE: Single-bitted

Gold-Sniffers

GOLD-SNIFFERS ARE HANDY GADGETS...but not absolutely necessary as long as you work mainly dry-ground areas. But, if you find water seeping into the places you are cleaning out, or if you attempt to clean out crevices located under water...the gold-sniffer will usually mean the difference between beans or steak on the table. They come in all sorts of sizes and shapes; home-made and ready-made, little ones and big ones.

They are, however, all about the same in principle, being simple, hand-held suction-dredges that "inhale" the gold particles up out of water-filled crevices...and deposit them safely within inner compartments of the sniffer. They can be purchased at most of the larger prospectors' equipment shops...or they can be easily made by almost anyone.

A bulk-type caulking gun, or certain types of grease-guns — fitted with flexible snouts — make good sniffers. They are sturdy, and when the handles are pulled up with a quick snap, they develop considerable suction power. Such sniffers do have one big drawback; they are heavy!

Lighter sniffers can be made with a rubber, battery-filler bulb, a piece of rigid tubing, a rubber stopper and a short piece of small rubber hose. The drawing below shows the construction details of a typical, home-made, bulb-type sniffer. The rubber bulb must be firm, able to create strong suction.

RUBBER, VACUUM-BULB
GOLD SNIFFER

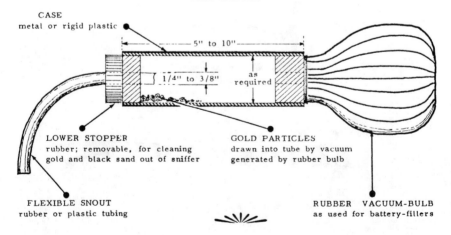

CASE
metal or rigid plastic

5" to 10"

1/4" to 3/8"

as required

LOWER STOPPER
rubber; removable, for cleaning
gold and black sand out of sniffer

GOLD PARTICLES
drawn into tube by vacuum
generated by rubber bulb

FLEXIBLE SNOUT
rubber or plastic tubing

RUBBER VACUUM-BULB
as used for battery-fillers

Mercury, Magnifying Glasses, Gold-Bottles

MERCURY IS USEFUL...sometimes permitting you to save gold you might otherwise lose. With it you can save a much higher percentage of the fine gold that usually washes out of your gold pan unless you are being exceedingly careful. Unless you really get bitten by the prospecting "bug"...from four to eight ounces are about all that you are apt to need during a whole summer's panning. Mercury can be purchased from chemical and prospectors' supply houses and from many drug stores. Handle it carefully and pack it well; the very weight of mercury causes it to break storage bottles with no more than a light shock.

MAGNIFYING GLASSES are not absolutely necessary, but they are handy to have along with you. The stacked-lens type, having two or more individual lenses, swivel mounted in a plastic or metal case, is the best. The big, reading-glass type isn't really powerful enough, and they are too fragile and cumbersome. Even your littlest pieces of gold will take on new glamor when you look at them through a 10-power glass!

GOLD-BOTTLE, as a name, isn't as romantic-sounding as "leather-poke," but bottles are a whole lot more practical. The type of glass or plastic bottles used for prescription medicines will do just fine. Screw-type tops are best, but if you should use the friction-top type, be careful; be sure that the top fits tightly. Keep your bottle filled with water when you have gold in it. Not only does the water keep you from losing particles of gold when you open the bottle...your gold looks ever so much bigger in a water-filled bottle! In case you're not particularly interested in looking at your gold (*is there such a person?*), the plastic containers that some 35MM film now comes in are good; the seals are tight enough even to hold flour gold.

HOW TO PAN GOLD

Basic Facts For The Gold Panner

YOUR DESIRE TO BE SUCCESSFUL at your gold panning must be accompanied by your willingness to learn certain, basic facts concerning gold...because these facts generally hold true wherever placer gold is mined. These basic facts can well be compared with the foundation of a building: Necessary, if the structure is to stand and endure. So, do learn these basic facts about panning for gold. You will increase by a thousand-fold your chances of consistently coming home with gold in your poke!

Basic Fact No. 1: — GOLD IS HEAVY

● *Placer gold is heavier than the sands and gravels in which it is found.* For this reason, it is technically quite simple to separate the gold from the sand and gravel. This "heaviness" is caused by the density of the metal and a natural force called "gravity." All placer mining operations are dependent upon the force of gravity...not only for the recovery methods themselves, but for the manner in which the gold was distributed and concentrated in the streams in the first place.

● The difference in heaviness between gold and the sands and gravels is the reason why flowing water and agitation cause gold to work its way down through the lighter materials (the sands and gravels), toward the bottoms of rivers and streams...and of sluice boxes and gold-pans.

● Being heavy, gold has a tendency to bunch up or concentrate when certain conditions exist...and in certain kinds of places. The conditions generally concern the ability of the water-flow to keep the gold-sand-gravel mass moving on down the stream. The places generally concern natural or artificial obstructions to the movement.

Basic Fact No. 2: — WORK WHERE GOLD IS TO BE FOUND

● *If there is no gold in the sand and gravel...there will be no gold in the pan.* To list this statement as a Basic Fact might seem ridiculous...because it is such an obviously elementary conclusion. But, the wasted efforts of scores of beginners prove that the statement is not as obvious as you would think. So remember, you must work where gold is to be found — in sufficient quantities — if you intend to make money with your gold-panning!

● Avoid panning in ground that has been worked by every Tom, Dick and

Harry for a hundred years or more...unless you don't mind working for pennies a day! You can depend upon the fact that the easier a piece of ground is to get to...the more times it has been looked over and worked.

● Whenever possible, prospect in the little streams. Hunt for pockets that have been overlooked and for places that appear to have been unworked for many years. Be patient and observe with care. Cover the ground slowly... because these places won't be big. Keep it firmly in your mind that a bedrock crack just one-eighth of an inch wide by two feet long can easily hold several hundred dollars worth of gold!

Basic Fact No. 3: — PANS ARE FOR "POT-HOLES"

● *If you want to make money with your pan...confine your work to "sniping," "pot-holing," and "crevicing."* These old miner's terms all mean about the same thing; the extra-careful searching for and cleaning out of bedrock cracks, pot-holes and crevices in gold-bearing streams.

● You cannot make money trying to work gravel-bars (even small ones!) with your pan. Stick to the bedrock mining. It will save you a lot of wasted effort, sore muscles and discouragement.

Basic Fact No. 4: — HUNT THE BIGGER PIECES

● *One piece of gold the size of a grain of rice contains more gold, by weight, than all the flour gold you are apt to save in a hard day's panning!* And, even a piece that size will buy more conversation than beans and bacon. The tiny flecks of gold we call flour can be found in almost every stream in the West. Five or ten of these flecks in a beginner's pan..."*Hot ziggety!*" Right away he figures he's struck it rich! The reality is, of course, that even though they shine so enticingly in your pan, even though they sparkle and glisten like fireworks, most are so tiny you couldn't buy a cup of coffee with a thousand of them! (Especially at the price of coffee today!)

● Unless you are panning just for the exercise and really have no desire for gold in your poke, look for the places where the larger grains and bits are most likely to be found. This isn't necessarily the case when working large volumes of ground with a sluice box — and there are some good placers that contain only fine gold — but, for the most part, the bigger pieces of gold provide your main hope of profit from panning.

General Panning Instructions

EOPLE DO NOT HANDLE their gold pans just alike...so don't worry if you don't seem to do it as you have seen others handle their pans. There is no one-and-only way to load the pan, to wet down the material loaded into the pan, to break up the lumps and pick out the rocks, to slough off the worthless materials...the sands, gravels and black sand. And further there is no one-and-only way to get gold out of a pan...and to take care of the pan itself. If you can work down a pan of material quickly and save the gold that's in it, you are doing it right no matter what anyone tries to tell you! Every set of instructions for panning gold should therefore, in my opinion, be confined to a generalized outline that demonstrates principles more than exacting, precise techniques. That is the reason the instructions in this book explain the "why" in considerable detail...and the "how" in a manner that is flexible enough to allow for many variations of situations and conditions.

The person who can work off the worthless material from a gold-pan quickly and, at the same time, save almost all of the gold...definitely understands how gold acts when it is agitated in a water-sand-gravel mixture. And *you* should understand it by now...as many times as I have repeated myself! Any person that loses most of the gold is either innocent of basic gold-savvy... or is simply as impatient as all get-out, and a little careless to boot.

The general instructions given below will put you on the right track...for understanding and utilizing the procedures outlined in the next chapter.

GENERAL INSTRUCTIONS FOR THE BEGINNER

● Pick out your panning-spot. You will want a place where the water is deep enough to cover your loaded pan, and where the water flows fast enough to move the muddy water from your pan on out of the way. The water should not be moving swiftly, however, as the pressure against the pan is apt to cause you to lose control...or, to sweep the contents of your pan right out into the stream...*and that's bad!*

● You will always have better control of the pan when you are seated... and you won't get so tired. Fix a place where you can sit down to do your panning! *You'll find it easier on both your back and your disposition!*

● Don't load too much material into your pan. From one-half to two-third's full is plenty...while you are learning.

● Make sure that every bit of material in the pan gets thoroughly wetted, that clay and soil lumps are dissolved, that roots and mosses are vigorously swished about in the water (over the pan, of course!), and that the rocks are washed clean. Use your hands to squeeze and work the roots and moss, and to break up the clay and soil lumps.

● Pick out all the rocks and pieces of material that are larger than small marbles. Don't try to wash them out over the lip of your pan. (Remember Fact No. 5! It takes plenty of water-power to force the bigger, heavier pieces of rock out of the pan...enough power to take the gold right along with the rocks.) The clay and soil particles will run out of the pan as muddy water; the sand and small pieces of gravel will slough off over the lip of the pan.

For your practice panning, using the detailed procedures given in the next chapter, get a number of pieces of small lead shot. Partially flatten a few of them. Put a definite number of pieces into your pan, say ten or twelve. Then, load your pan about half-full of ordinary river gravel. At this point, don't worry about whether or not it has any gold in it. You are simply learning how to use your pan...using a pre-determined quantity of lead shot in the pan for checking the progress of your panning efficiency.

Work off the material until you have only a half of a cup or less of the heavier concentrates left in the pan. Next, count the shot still left. Continue this practice until you can easily save whatever shot you put in your pan. After you have mastered this part of your training, which you should be able to do in an hour or so...begin again, using much smaller shot. Either cut the shot that you have into little bits and pieces, or get some that are small enough. Practice with this small shot until you can save it without any strain.

For the final phase of this part of your training, begin to increase your speed until you are panning at a comfortable but sufficiently rapid rate...while at the same time, you are saving the shot that you put into your pan. This particular phase will probably require at least one full day, and for those people who have trouble coordinating their muscular responses it will take much longer. In the event that you feel practice to be something for the "other fellow", let me remind you that you won't be able to save any reasonable part of the gold that you put into your pan if you can't save the smaller shot particles. And, you'll never know whether or not you can...unless you actually do this controlled-loading panning practice.

Specific Procedures: Steps 1 Through 7

NOW THAT YOU HAVE LEARNED the six important Gold Facts... and now that you have mastered the general instructions about panning, you are ready to go about working off an actual panful of material. To get that material, you have shoveled away the low-pay sand and gravel overburden from a bit of promising-looking bedrock; you have carefully cleaned out one of the crevices with your crevicing-tools, spoon and brush; you have scraped up the patch of moss that was growing like a little green carpet by the crevice, and you have carefully brushed into your pan the dried silt and sand that was under the moss. And further, you have already selected the best panning spot by the stream. The water is perhaps six inches deep and flowing just fast enough to keep the muddy panning water out of your way; the bottom is fairly level, so that you can set your pan down from time to time without tipping it too much. There is also a place where you can sit down in some comfort, while you pan! While you didn't actually see any nuggets in the material as you loaded it into your pan, you have the feeling that this half-a-pan of carefully selected material has gold in it...and you want it! Here is how you go about getting it:

STEP NO. 1: – Wet The Material Thoroughly

● Put your pan, loaded with materials, down into your panning hole...just deeply enough so that everything is submerged under water.

● Give the pan several vigorous shakes back and forth and from side to side *(not so vigorously that you slosh any of the material out of the pan!).*

● Change from the shaking motion to a gentle twirling movement, so that the material starts revolving in a circle in the pan. For most right-handed persons, the easiest direction of rotation is counter-clockwise. During this time, most of the dirt and clay will start to break up, and will run out of the pan as muddy water.

STEP NO. 2: – Throw Out The Large Rocks And Moss

● Put the pan down, on the bottom of your panning-hole. Work the material with your fingers to break up the lumps and to squeeze out the roots and moss.

● Swish the roots and moss vigorously in the water, then throw them out.

● Throw out the large rocks, after making sure that they are washed clean.

STEP NO. 3: — Throw Out The Small Rocks

● Pick up the pan, just a bit, keeping everything under water. Again shake the pan back and forth, from side to side, and rotate the material with the twirling movement. This should just about finish breaking up the soil and clay lumps. When the water no longer flows out muddy, you know that the soil and clay are about gone.

● Set the pan down again and pick out the larger rocks.

● Pick up the pan: Shake it and twirl it; set it down and pick out rocks. You will probably have to do this three or four times in order to get rid of all the rocks that are larger than small marbles.

With a little practice, you will be able to tell when you have gotten rid of all the above material and are ready to start sloughing off the finer material, the sand, gravel, etc., so you can get to your gold.

STEP NO. 4: — Slough Off The Sand And Gravel

● With the pan under water, you tip it just a little, so that the lip of the pan farthest from you is an inch or two lower than the nearer one. The exact angle of this tilt isn't too important, but...if you tilt the pan too much, you risk losing your gold; if you don't tilt it enough, it's hard to slough off the waste material. Practice will teach you more about this part of your panning than the reading of 15 books. In any event, the lip of the pan — on the down-tilted side — should always be higher than the junction-point of the pan's bottom and rim, in order to keep the gold from sliding out.

Now, you are ready for the sloughing-off process. Any 6-year-old child can easily do the panning up to this point without losing a bit of gold. Here begins the part that separates the men from the boys; here is where the impatient or careless panner loses his gold.

● Begin to swirl the water from side to side with a slight forward-tossing motion, carefully, but with sufficient force to move the topmost sand and gravel particles out toward the lowest edge of the pan...and on out over the lip. To describe this motion is harder than to do it. To describe it is to make it sound complicated...but it is really very simple. Because of the side-to-side swirling motion of the water, the particles of sand and gravel do not move in a straight line toward the lower lip. Instead, they move more in a series of little diagonals.

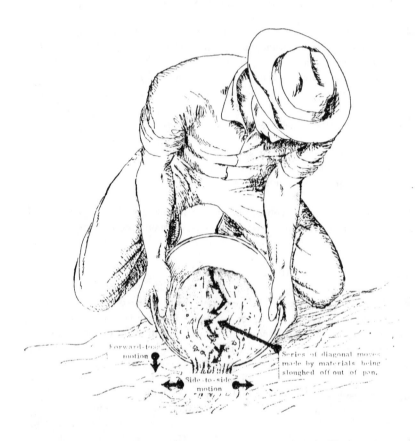

Forward-to motion

Side-to-side motion

Series of diagonal moves made by materials being sloughed off out of pan.

● Level the pan a bit from time to time, and shake it back and forth and from side to side. The reason for this should be obvious to you by now: you are keeping the gold down on the bottom of your pan. (*Remember Basic Fact Nos. 1 and 2!*) Continue this routine until there is only about two cupfuls of the heavier material left in your pan. This material is usually called "concentrate." At this point, it is wise to check your pan for nuggets and pieces that you can pick out by hand.

Incidentally, some panners do not use the twirling technique described above. Instead, they use a simple series of raising and lowering motions that cause a rather strong in-flow and out-flow of water. The out-flowing water sloughs the worthless materials off out of the pan. This technique is simpler and is perhaps a bit faster. But, personally, I believe that beginners are apt to lose too much of their gold by using it.

STEP NO. 5: — Slough Off The Black Sand

At this point, it is better procedure for the beginner to raise the pan completely out of the water...leaving about a half an inch of water in it. Raising your pan out of the water helps to eliminate the possibility of some sudden rushing swirl of the current washing out the contents of your pan.

● Tilt down the farthest rim of the pan enough to enable you to slough off the concentrates, using the twirling, tossing motion that you used in Step No. 4.

● Continue to slough off the concentrates, dipping the pan into the stream as often as necessary to keep water in it. Too much water is hard to control; not enough water makes it difficult to slough off the concentrates. Usually, from five to seven dips into the stream will do the job...if you're sloughing off as much material with each movement as you should.

● Stop the sloughing-off procedure when you have only three or four tablespoonfuls of residual concentrate left in your pan. The exact make-up of this residual concentrate will depend upon the stream you're working. Every mining area has its own percentages of black sands, pyrites, spent lead-shot, beer can openers, rusty nails...and gold.

STEP NO. 6: — Check The Pan For Gold

You are now ready to check your pan...to see whether or not you caught any "goodies" in it.

● Dip about a cupful of water into the pan, then raise it well up out of the water. Swirl the water around the pan a time or two, to spread the concentrates across it. Any nuggets or pieces will show up immediately and should be removed, with your tweezers, from the pan and put into your gold-bottle.

● Now, to check for fines and small bits of gold, tilt the far edge of the pan downward, just a bit, and gently shake the concentrate back and forth. This will deposit the concentrates at the far edge and will cause the gold to "string" out along the junction-point of the pan's bottom and rim.

● Tilt the pan back, the other way, with the low edge near you. Using a gentle, circular motion, begin to swirl the water slowly around and around the edge of the pan's bottom. The concentrates will begin to follow the water and, being lighter than the gold, the black sands will move along first. The gold will come last...stretching out in a little line or "string" of gold particles. It should take just a few of these circular motions to expose your gold.

STEP NO. 7: — Getting Your Gold Out Of The Pan

● At this point, you must decide how you are going to get the fines out of your pan. If there are just a few bits of flour or flecks, you can pick them out with your tweezers and put them right into your gold-bottle. If there are quite a few pieces of flour, you will save time and gold by putting the whole works — black sand, pyrites, gold and all — into another "catch-bottle" for clean-up at a later time, possibly with the use of mercury.

Some people carry a small, powerful magnet with them that they use for removing black sand from the flour gold. Such magnets are all right for removing magnetite, but they don't do much good with the hematite sands. In order to use a magnet for removing the black sands from the flour, first put your concentrates into your gold pan, then pour off as much of the water as possible. Let the concentrates dry out thoroughly, then pass the magnet slowly over the top of them. The magnet should be quite close to the black sands so that they will jump up onto it, leaving the flour gold behind in the pan. Clean the accumulations of black sand from the magnet by scraping and wiping it with your hands.

Personally, I think that magnets are, at best, a mediocre compromise as a means of separating the black sands from your flour gold. Tweezers are faster for just a few flecks...and mercury is not only faster, it is a much surer way of separating large amounts. Not *safer*, just *surer!*

You can depend upon the fact that, from reading these few instructions, you haven't learned all there is to know about finding and panning gold...not by a long sight. But, armed with these facts, you certainly can go out into a stream and, if gold is there, you'll at least be able to find some of it. After practicing the panning technique included in these Seven Steps, you'll be able to save most of the gold that you put *into* your pan...and these are "steps" in the right direction!

I don't pretend that the Seven Steps make up the whole story of handling a gold-pan...or that my Six Fundamental Facts represent the sum of all knowledge on prospecting. There is more to the art of finding and panning gold than could ever be written into a whole library of books...if all the possible combinations of situations and conditions are taken into consideration. But, the Six Facts and the Seven Steps are complete enough for your primary learning process, and practice at prospecting and panning will provide your "graduation exercises!"

The drawing shown below illustrates how gold and heavy concentrates collect on the bottom of a gold-pan. It is important for you to keep agitating your pan enough to keep the gold down on the bottom. You can also see how tipping the pan too much creates the hazard of having your gold slide right out of the pan. Remember: 1) **Agitate**; to keep the gold on the bottom of your pan. 2) **Enough tilt**; so that the worthless materials can be sloughed off out of the pan. 3) **Not too much tilt**; so that you lose your gold...right out over the lip of your pan.

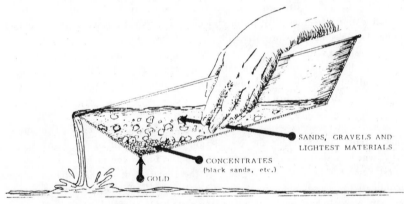

SANDS, GRAVELS AND LIGHTEST MATERIALS

CONCENTRATES
(black sands, etc.)

GOLD

Here is another way that you can lose gold out of your pan, a way that costs many a beginner and careless panner most of the gold they manage to get into their pans. It happens like this: 1) *A bit too much tilt to the pan,* and, 2) *A dab too much forward-toss movement.* Suddenly, the entire contents of the pan will slide forward a bit, toward the lip of the pan...and some part, including concentrates, will be lost. Do this more than just a few times while working off a panful of material and all you'll get for your efforts will be a backache!

MORE USEFUL INFORMATION

Your Legal Rights To Pan Gold

THERE ARE STILL LOTS OF PLACES where you can legally prospect and use your gold pan. In the western States — in the very areas where placer gold has been found in the most abundant quantities — there are millions of acres of land still in the Public Domain. And, while more and more restrictions are being placed upon where you may enter and what you may do when there, most of the Public Domain land is still open for mineral exploration...at least by hobbyists and vacationers. You may for the most part prospect upon such open land, with or without filing a mining claim, as you wish.

If you should find a good prospect while panning — one you feel worthy of further development and working — then by all means post your legal discovery notice as required by law as quickly as possible. Then register your claim with the recorder of the county in which your discovery is located. When the Feds move in to make their takeover complete, as they obviously intend to do unless stopped, you will have to register your claim in some Federal office...if, indeed, you will still be "allowed" the privilege of mining Public Domain lands. Currently, the laws, rules and regulations governing mineral resources and mining claims vary somewhat, from State to State. Protect yourself against making embarrassing or expensive mistakes by getting (and studying!) copies of the laws from the bureau of mines of the State where you will be prospecting.

When you prospect and pan within the boundaries of the Public Domain, you currently come under the jurisdiction of the Bureau of Land Management; when in the National Forests, you are also under the jurisdiction of the Forest Service. The first is an agency of the Department of the Interior; the second, of the Department of Agriculture. If you think these two see eye to eye, you haven't had your education completed. Overriding both, now, is the Environmental Protection Agency...with powers so broad they are frightening. In most States, you are also under the jurisdiction of the fish and game commissions; in places, of the various soil conservation districts. Then, there are the many water-control and park commissions...and neither last nor least, you are always subject to fire-control regulations. Furthermore, even the public utilities join in the efforts continuously being made to increase the restrictions being placed upon what you may and may not do on and within the Public Domain...by pushing for the enactment of regulations that are advantageous mainly to them.

Once you proceed beyond the realm of the relatively simple yet straight-

Roy Lagal, demonstrating how to use a detector to locate black sand pockets along a stream bank — and, thereby, possible concentrations of placer gold. Even gold far too fine to be directly detectable by the instrument can usually be found by this method. Should nuggets large enough to be located by the detector be present within the scanning area, they can be found with the instrument. When using a plastic pan, such as the Gravity-Trap pan shown, the operator can easily determine whether or not detected nuggets have been shoveled into the pan simply by scanning the pan with the detector. This can save considerable panning time and effort! The instrument being used here is a Garrett Master Hunter (BFO), 1974 model, equipped with waterproof, dual 3½'' and 6½'' coil system. This combination provides dependability, good depth and easy pin-pointing capability.

Karl von Mueller: 1970

Karl von Mueller and Wally MacLaren, working one of the high-altitude gold placers in Colorado's Rocky Mountains. The dredge is a Sparton, the detector is a Garrett Master Hunter (BFO)...the same make, model and year of my most-trusted, most-used, all-purpose unit.

E.S. LeGaye: 1974

A.M. Stagner, demonstrating a Garrett Gravity Trap gold pan. This new, efficient pan is one of the few modern-day plastic devices good enough to survive her experienced, critical testing and win approval. Using this pan, Mrs. Stagner recovered a surprising amount of very fine flour gold from black sand concentrates already carefully panned with a standard steel pan. She says, ''I didn't expect to like it, but I do. It's really good!''

forward and common-sense General Mining Law of 1872 — the basic, clear-cut set of laws that yet regulate mineral exploration and mining rights on lands located within the Public Domain — you enter a jungle of jurisdictional over-lappings, departmental and agency ambitions, legal confusion...and rules and regulations issued on one level of administration that are all too often coun-termanded by those issued on other levels. For years now, professional miners have been harassed to such an unreasonable extent by the various custodial agencies that one is almost forced to this conclusion: for whatever reason, the officials of those bureaucratic empires consider prospecting and mining to be some sinister, heinous crime against America...an evil to be stamped out at whatever cost (to the taxpayers, of course!).

But, within the scope of activities yet permitted you by the above-mentioned (and other!) regulatory agencies, all lands owned in the name of the U.S. Government are open for your prospecting and panning (at least on the hobby, recreational level) — whether surveyed or unsurveyed, including the beds of unnavigable streams — except certain exclusions which include but are not limited to:

Private property; municipal, county and state lands; valid mining claims and mining and millsite patents; most power sites and water reservoir reser-vations; the beds of navigable streams, lake beds permanently covered by water, and land situated below mean high tide; National Parks, National Lakes and Seashores, National Historic Sites, Wilderness Areas and Monuments; mili-tary and Indian reservations; and certain Spanish land grants. There are some exceptions (and supplements!) to the above, but in a most general sense, it is about the way things are.

In case you are thinking, *"There is nothing left...no place at all for me to prospect and pan!"*...let me remind you that there are about 140,000,000 acres of land lying within the National Forests alone. In California, for example, over 20% of the total land area of that State is located within the boundaries of 17 National Forests. On June 30, 1960, the General Services Administration reported that the Federal Government owned 771,000,000 acres of land in the United States...an utterly fantastic 33.9% of the land area of the nation! Out of this total, almost 725,000,000 acreas are in 12 gold-bearing western States. Yes...*there is* — *at least at this writing* — *plenty of land left for you to roam over and prospect!*

How To Use Mercury

WHILE IT IS ALWAYS BEST to avoid the use of mercury in both pans and sluice boxes (for several valid reasons), there are times when its use can be almost an absolute must if you wish to save gold. For example, when the gold is mostly in the form of flour and very fine particles, mercury will help you separate the gold from the waste material faster and more surely...especially when the material being worked includes large quantities of black sand. *(That stuff can be a holy terror in pans and sluice boxes!)* Here are some important facts about mercury...a liquid metal that is both valuable servant and potential assassin:

Mercury has an intense affinity for gold and for certain other metals, such as silver and copper. When mercury comes into contact with clean particles of gold, therefore, the particles become superficially coated with and/or combined with the mercury...according to particle size, thickness and mass. When two or more such affected particles and clumps of particles come into contact with each other within liquid mercury, they become loosely cemented or "chemically-soldered" together. Such an aggregation of mercury coated and cemented particles is called "amalgam"...and the process of bringing them together is called "amalgamation". The cemented particles become — in a practical sense — parts of much larger wholes and, therefore, far heavier than the individual, tiny particles. The resultant clumps are more easily retained in your pan or sluice box.

Now, *here are some good reasons for not using mercury:* When most of the gold in the ground you are working is already in larger particles, bits, pieces and nuggets — the weight-equivalents of mercury-cemented clumps — avoid the use of mercury as if it were the plague! With careful panning and sluicing techniques, it is not needed to save coarse gold. Not only is it a serious threat to health and life, mercury spoils the "natural state" appearance of your gold. Only by refining can all mercury be separated from gold. So... *why risk your health and life when there is no need?* And...*why risk spoiling a beautiful nugget by contaminating it with mercury when there is no need?*

HOW TO AMALGAMATE:—

If practical realities require that you use mercury, here is how to bring about an amalgamation of mercury and your gold: 1) Accumulate your gold-laden black sand concentrates as you pan (or work your sluice box). Any water-tight container will do. When you have enough, 2) Put about a third or half a pan of the concentrates into a gold pan that is absolutely free of all oils and greases. 3) Add enough water to saturate and cover the concentrate mass at least half an inch. 4) Pour an ounce or two of mercury into the pan. 5) Shake the pan briskly from side to side, then around and around in a twirling, swirling motion for a few moments. This action should be brisk enough to enable the mercury and the gold particles to sink to the bottom of the mass...but not so brisk that you slosh out your gold-laden concentrates!

This action breaks the mercury apart into countless droplets, globules and little pools...thereby enhancing contact between mercury and gold particles. After some moments, 6) begin to slough off the lighter parts of the concentrates. As this sloughing-off proceeds, be sure to agitate the pan from time to time. This helps keep the mercury and gold down on the bottom of the pan, and allows maximum opportunity for "weddings" between gold and mercury.

It isn't necessary to get rid of all the black sand. Just slough off enough so (a) you can consolidate the mercury into a single pool or mass again, after all the gold has been picked up, and (b) you can get the gold-laden mercury out of the pan and into a suitable storage container. Since mercury tends to consolidate into pools anyway, this occurs almost automatically and simultaneously as you slough off the black sand.

During the panning, 7) test the concentrates occasionally for unamalgamated gold particles. This is easy when you know how: First, work the concentrate mass down into the lowered, far side of your pan (the side away from you); then tilt the pan until the lowest side is now nearest you. Shake the pan, carefully. If you have sloughed off enough of the black sand, the weight of the gold-laden mercury will cause it to slide out from under the concentrates and roll into a little pool at the low side, away from the concentrates. Next, swirl the water gently around the pan. (For most right-handed persons, a counter-clockwise rotation is easiest to master.) The water will move the black sand with it...and unamalgamated gold particles will show up in a little string along the far edge of the pan. When you can no longer see free gold, you are ready to remove the gold-laden mercury from the pan.

When you are satisfied that there is no more unamalgamated gold in your pan, 8) pour the gold-laden mercury into a container for later treatment to separate the gold from the mercury. It is fairly easy to pour the mercury out into a wide-mouth, glass catch-bottle...but even professional miners usually do it over another pan! The mercury can more readily be directed into the bottle if you place your two thumbs about an inch apart — pressed tightly against the rim of the pan — and thereby provide a channel through which the mercury can flow over the rim and safely into your catch-bottle. Don't fret if some water gets into the bottle, along with the mercury. It won't cause any trouble...and you will get rid of it during the next step. If you should have an accident and spill your gold-laden mercury onto the ground, don't despair! You can save all or most of it simply by digging up the soil where it fell and panning it.

RETORTING THE AMALGAM:—

When you are ready to separate your gold from the mercury, here is an easy way to do it...the way used by nearly every professional prospector and placer mine operator that I know:

1) Begin by laying a wet, first-quality fine chamois skin over the bottom of your gold pan...with the excess lapping over the rim. 2) Pour the gold-laden mercury out of the catch-bottle onto the chamois. 3) Carefully lift up the edges of the chamois, to form a sack or pouch...with the mercury inside. 4) With one hand hold the chamois pouch tightly, over the pan; 5) Begin to squeeze the pouch by twisting the lower part around and around, with the gold-laden mercury in a pool at the bottom of the pouch...as though you were wringing out a piece of laundry. As you twist, this will create more and more pressure on the mercury. 6) When the pressure gets great enough, the mercury — but practically none of the gold — will begin to extrude through the pores of the chamois in tiny droplets, and continue until almost all has escaped and dropped into the pan. A bit of care during this work is necessary. Too much pressure will cause the mercury to spurt through the chamois with considerable force — often several feet — and thereby be lost.

Knowing what I now do about the hazards inherent in handling mercury, I myself do this part entirely under water...using a large, plastic bucket. This not only avoids the possible loss of the extruded mercury, wet hands minimize the possibility of mercury absorption into the body. *(I sometimes shudder when I remember the casual manner with which I handled not only mercury but cyanide and dynamite those many years ago...when I was a youthfully eager but green-as-grass seeker of gold!)*

When you can no longer squeeze any mercury through the chamois, you are done with this part. Upon opening the chamois pouch, you will find a silver-colored ball of mercury-coated, tightly compressed gold particles...gold amalgam. This ball is called a "button" by most miners...and contains from 25% to 40% gold, by weight, depending upon size of particles, amount of compression, etc. Save the extruded mercury for re-use by pouring off the water; then pour the mercury into a storage container.

To remove the mercury which still remains on your gold, the button must be heated enough to vaporize and drive off the mercury. Even a small wood fire generates enough heat to do the job. *But remember, mercury fumes are highly toxic!* This work must be done in such a way that the fumes are confined and not allowed to escape into the atmosphere. Furthermore, since mercury is now quite expensive, it makes good, practical sense to utilize some device that will enable you not only to remove the mercury from your gold but to recover the mercury as a liquid, suitable for re-use.

Such a device is called a "retort" or "still"...and comes in many variations of design and efficiency. All have one important point in common, however: each receives gold-laden mercury, delivers gold back free of mercury, and recovers mercury for further use. A device (?) I saw being used in the California gold placers during the depression days of the early 1930's beats everything I've seen since for utter simplicity. (Not *foolproof*...but simple!) This "retort" was nothing more than one-half of a potato, a piece of sheet iron, and a small wood fire! Yet, made and used with reasonable care, such potato "retorts" can be almost as efficient at vaporizing the mercury off of the gold and re-distilling it for further use as commercially-made iron retorts.

Here is how to make and use a potato "retort": Cut a large potato in half, lengthwise (use care to make a smooth, straight cut that will provide as flat a surface as possible). In the flat side of one of the halves, notch out a cavity just a little bit bigger than your amalgam button. Place the button in the cavity, then turn the potato flat side down on a piece of sheet iron (a steel gold pan will do quite nicely).

Two points are important: 1) *The button should make physical contact with the iron, rather than be supported above it by the potato.* Why? Because the efficiency of vaporization and condensation of the mercury fumes is dependent upon the button being substantially hotter than the surrounding potato fibers, and, 2) *The flat side of the potato should make a tight seal with the sheet iron.* Why? Because the efficiency of mercury recovery -- and, possibly, your health or life! -- depends upon a vapor-proof seal at the junction of potato and sheet iron.

To help reduce mercury vapor leakage at the seal and through the potato, wrap a piece of aluminum foil over the outer, exposed part of the potato... keeping the edges high enough to avoid contact with the sheet iron. Then pack damp clay around the joint of potato and sheet iron, up onto the foil wrap. Sometimes gold tends to stick to the sheet iron when retorting, especially if the iron surface is rough. This can be eliminated by rubbing common chalk on the iron, where it contacts the button.

When all is ready, place the whole business — potato "retort", button, and sheet iron — on a rock or other support...out in the open air, well away from people and animals. Unless you really do know what you are doing (in a completely professional and trained sense), *never retort mercury inside a building...no matter how "well-ventilated"!* Light a small wood fire under the sheet iron; maintain the fire long enough and hot enough to cook the potato. During this time, the heat will vaporize the mercury and drive it off of the gold particles...into the somewhat cooler potato fibers. Here, the mercury fumes re-condense into liquid form and remain.

By the time the potato is cooked...the gold is clean! Lift off the cooked potato; you will find a ball of bright yellow gold lying on the sheet iron. In this form, gold is generally referred to as "sponge gold"...and usually remains in the ball form of the button. Place your gold in a safe place, then put the cooked potato and some water in a clean gold pan. Mash the potato into a thin slurry with a stick or stainless steel potato masher; add more water and rinse away the potato residue into another container. You will find most of your mercury still in the pan, bright and shiny...as good as new for catching gold. Pour the mercury into your storage container, then bury the water and potato particles...to eliminate possible mercury contamination of the stream water and prevent some animal or child from finding and eating the particles.

You need not worry about accidentally melting your gold when retorting this way. Wood burns at about 1000 degrees Fahrenheit; mercury vaporizes at 674 degrees, gold melts at 1945 degrees. Charcoal or large quantities of live wood-coals — plus forced air draft — is of course another matter. Use these and you will likely wind up with gold bullion instead of a gold button!

The foregoing represents but a tiny fraction of the available data on mercury, mercury amalgams and retorting, and the subject gets really technical when the treatment of complex mill ores are involved. For example, one of my favorite reference works on the milling of ores (*Text Book of Ore Dressing*, by Robert H. Richards, S.B., LL.D., McGraw-Hill, 1909) requires 24 pages of fine print to cover this one subject. But, fortunately, conditions are far simpler for gold panners and operators of small gold placers. For these folks, the main concerns are: a) Keeping the gold particles free of all oils and greases, b) Obtaining the maximum possible contact between gold particles and mercury, c.) Saving the maximum possible amounts of gold and mercury in sluice boxes, pans and catch-bottles, and d.) Safe handling techniques when using mercury.

SAFETY TIPS:—

Now, some useful information about this Jekyl and Hyde material...
mercury. Read it with care. The health and life you might thereby save could
very well be your own! *Remember this fact well: Mercury in all forms —
metallic and compounds — is always potentially dangerous, often deadly!* Wide
differences of opinion exist amongst equally-qualified toxicologists and medical doctors about the actual extent of dangers inherent in orally ingested
metallic mercury. But, they all agree upon the lethal capabilities of mercury
fumes and all mercury compounds.

Mercury combines with many inorganic and a few organic elements to
form a vast number of compounds...most of which are quite useful (and
toxic!) to man. Just a sampling includes: mercury, mercuric and mercurous
acetates, bromates and bromides, chlorates and chlorides, cyanides, nitrates
and oxides, azides, fulminates and nitrides, sulfates and sulfides, tartrates and
tungstates, etc. Yes, mercury is a valuable, beneficial element...a servant
capable of working hard in man's behalf, and of doing much good. But, at no
time is it a servant that can be handled carelessly without incurring great risk.

Mercury is a dense and therefore heavy metal (sp. gr. 13.546, at 68 degrees,
Fahrenheit), a fair conductor of electricity. It weighs 846 pounds per cubic
foot...70% less than gold, but 72½% more than iron. It is the only metal that is
liquid at ordinary temperatures. Mercury is a solid metal at temperatures
lower than —40 degrees, F., above which temperature it "melts" into the
silvery-white liquid form we are accustomed to seeing and using. It begins to
vaporize slightly at normal room temperatures, fumes quite briskly at 212
degees F., and boils away completely, as a vapor or fumes, at 674 degrees, F.
Because mercury does vaporize at room temperatures, open containers of the
metal in a dwelling pose serious health threats. Therefore, *always keep mercury stored in vessels with tight-fitting covers. Even in very small amounts,
mercury can do appalling, often irreversible damage to living beings. To you,
for example, or to your family!*

Inhaling even very small amounts of mercury fumes and absorbing metallic mercury through the skin or mucous membranes can result in erethism (an
abnormal state of excitement, irritability, fatigue and headache), tremor, sali-
vation, and serious corrosive damage to mucous membranes of nose, mouth
and throat, and to lung tissues. Just a bit more exposure can add loss of teeth
and grave damage to your gastrointestinal tract and central nervous system.
This level of absorption also threatens you with pneumonitis, bronchitis,
severe chest pains and dyspnea (an unpleasant form of breathing difficulties).

Long-continued, multiple exposures at this level virtually guarantees you years of misery...of half-life.

And...*in lethal doses* (not very large amounts, actually!), *inhaled mercury fumes and metallic mercury absorbed by the body will cause your death – generally from nephritis and consequent kidney failure – usually within 10 days.* If you have any tendency to carelessness or bravado...think a bit about these facts! They should sober all but the suicide-bent.

Here is an additional danger factor involving mercury. Books on first-aid seldom mention treatments for metallic mercury and its fumes, nor do most "home remedy" medical text books. *Even the very best of clinical toxicological references contain but a surprisingly small number of recommendations for emergency treatment of mercury fume poisoning*...and, book to book, there is little agreement on preferred treatments.

However, the following procedure seems generally acceptable to most toxicologists and medical doctors as a "first" aid treatment: 1) *Drink the whites of three or more eggs;* this will convert at least a part of the mercury to inert albuminate of mercury. 2) *Chew and swallow some activated charcoal tablets;* this material helps absorb mercury and its compounds. 3) *Drink a quart or more of milk or half-and-half cream;* this will help coat the mucous linings of the mouth, throat and stomach. 4) *Induce vomiting;* inhaled mercury fumes can distill into metallic, liquid mercury in the mouth and throat, to be swallowed into the stomach. Vomiting will help remove such distilled metal from the body. 5) *Use saline cathartics, but not strong purges;* this will help to remove mercury from the intestines and lower bowels. And, most important, since none of the above may have helped one iota, 6) *Get to a good doctor or first class hospital as quickly as possible.*

My warnings about mercury's capacity to harm you add up to a rather gruesome bit of reading, true. But, they aren't intended to frighten you entirely away from using mercury as a valuable, oft-times necessary tool for recovering fine gold. With reasonable precautions and prudent handling, mercury can be as safe to use as distilled water. And, for a fact, we all use many things every day even more dangerous to life and limb...our automobiles, for example. Treat mercury with considered respect, observe adequate safety precautions concerning handling and use, ventilation and disposal...then, you should never have a moment's trouble with it.

Weighing Your Take

AFTER THE PROSPECTING, after the hard work of digging and panning, after you have gotten your flecks, bits, pieces and chunks of gold safely into your catch-bottle...and after you have looked at them *(and looked and looked!)*, you will quite naturally begin to wonder just how much gold you have and what it is worth. The following information about how gold is weighed and valued will help fill that need. To begin, gold is usually weighed (for value-determination) on scales which are calibrated in the troy system of ounces and pounds...a system somewhat different from the avoirdupois system scales used by, for example, your butcher when he weighs your meat (and his thumb?). The unit of weight called a "grain" is the only one common to both troy and avoirdupois systems. The "grain" weighs precisely 0.064798918 gram (in the metric system). The significant difference between the troy and avoirdupois systems is in the number of grains required to make an ounce...and in the number of ounces required to make a pound.

In the troy system:

1 grain	equals	64.798918 metric milligrams
24 grains	equal	1.00 pennyweight
20 pennyweights	equal	1.00 ounce
12 ounces	equal	1.00 pound

In the troy system, there are 480 grains per ounce...and 12 ounces to the pound; a total of 5760 grains. In the avoirdupois system, there are 437.5 grains per ounce...and 16 ounces per pound; a total of 7000 grains. In other words, an avoirdupois pound is heavier than a troy pound by 1240 grains. If you weigh gold upon a scale calibrated in the avoirdupois system (the one commonly used by business, in the U.S.), you must multiply the indicated avoirdupois weight by the following factors in order to determine the correct, troy weight:

1 ounce (avoir.)	equals	0.911458 ounce	(troy)
1 pound (avoir.)	equals	14.58337 ounces	(troy)
1 pound (avoir.)	equals	1.21528 pounds	(troy)

To change troy weight to avoirdupois weight:

1 ounce (troy)	equals	1.09714 ounces	(avoir.)
1 pound (troy)	equals	13.16528 ounces	(avoir.)
1 pound (troy)	equals	0.82286 pound	(avoir.)

Whatever the market price for gold, value depends not only upon weight but upon purity of the metal. As purity decreases from 1000-fine, value decreases proportionately. In some instances, the alloying metals are paid for by the refiner, silver, for example. In other instances, alloying metals are not only not paid for, extra refining charges are tacked on as penalties, due to the refining difficulties they produce. The following table lists some values for gold of differing purities...weighed both, troy and avoirdupois (using $35 per troy ounce of 1000-fine gold as the value-base).

Troy:	1000-fine	900-fine	800-fine
1 grain	$000.073	$000.066	$000.058
1 pennyweight	1.75	1.58	1.40
1 ounce	35.00	31.50	28.00
1 pound	420.00	378.00	336.00
Avoirdupois:			
1 grain	000.073	000.066	000.058
1 ounce	31.90	28.71	25.52
1 pound	510.41	459.36	408.32

The scale used for weighing gold is called a balance. To be of any practical value, it must be sensitive enough to detect and measure weight differences of 1 grain or less (0.0020833 troy ounce), and sturdy enough to support at least 5 troy ounces of total weight. The simplest method of weighing your gold is to take it to licensed gold buyers and let them do it. But, if you really get bitten by the "gold bug"...you're going to want a balance of your own. You can, of course, make a workable balance...if you are mechanically minded and have both the time and the equipment. But, even at today's prices, you can buy a hand-held balance at most laboratory and prospectors' supply houses for less than $5, and a stand-type, for less than $10. A set of student-standard troy weights should cost less than $10. So...$15 or $20 — *and some gold!* — will put you in business!

BALANCE: Hand-held, student-type, satisfactory for prospecting trips

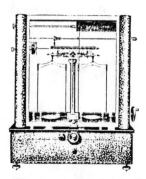

BALANCE: Precision, accurate to 1/20 mg., for laboratory use

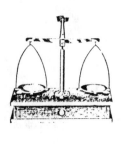

BALANCE: Stand-type, Adequate for field-measurements

CONCLUSION

Gold Is More Than Mere Metal

TREMENDOUS RESURGENCE OF INTEREST, and a ground-swell of deeply-felt emotions in everything "Old West" has come into being during the past 10 or 15 years. Not just in cowboys and Indians, wide-open spaces and scenic grandeur but — instead — in every kind of authentic memento of those days of greater courage, confidence and virility that once were ours as a growing nation...and which seem to have diminished greatly during the past 60 or 70 years.

It is obvious (to all who will but take the trouble to observe with care!) that vast numbers of our people — young and old — are growing progressively more depressed by dark forebodings about the current course of events and deteriorating quality of life. They grow more and more disillusioned by today's computerized depersonalizations, by ever-increasing regimentation of human beings by hordes of self-serving "Big Brother" politicians and bureaucrats, by the incessant probings into the complex, awesome unknowns of the infinitesimally-small world of atoms and the infinitely-vast expanse that is the universe...and by the constant barrages of ridicule and scorn directed at them from all sides by both the venal and the naive, who condemn virtually every established ethical value and standard of conduct.

Consequently, increasing numbers of our people seek out everything of authentic historic value and meaning...as though to satisfy some desperate, gnawing hunger for fresh inspiration, revitalized faith in our beginnings, and renewed courage to understand the present and face the future. In short — and in spite of the scorn heaped upon them by vacant-minded cynics who label them "nostalgia freaks" — they need and actively seek tangible evidence of life-purpose and life-continuity. And they hunt for and accumulate all sorts of articles, relics and artifacts...mementos that in some manner evoke the spirit — the *Zeitgeist* — of earlier, more robust times.

And there were such times...before we as a people traded away so much of our personal integrity, dignity and responsibility in exchange for the some-thing-for-nothing illusions and pap of cradle-to-grave "security" dispensed by our self-proclaimed all-wise, all-benevolent politicians and bureaucrats. *Raw gold — in fact, gold in most forms — is such a memento!*

Yes, gold — especially in the form of nuggets and gold-rich specimen-quartz — is an integral, vital part of the Western Heritage of these United States of America. It was the lure and the reality of gold that sparked a large part of the exploration of the West...and it was gold that provided much of the financial "muscle" that made possible the settlement and development of the Western States. In short, it was the lure of gold — as well as the opportunity to find free land and to enjoy freedom of personal expression — that led to the reality of this America of ours that does indeed stretch "...*from sea to shining sea!*"

Because of this fact, gold — especially raw, natural-state gold — has values that must be measured by other than by the yardsticks of mere utilitarian and monetary values. Gold has deeply-symbolic, valid historic values as well! It is a virtually indestructible symbol of the pride and courage, the grim determination, unsparing labors and ingenious resourcefulness — the well-nigh incredible accomplishments — of the early-day pioneers and settlers of the American West!

It is our good fortune today that, as hard-working and persistent as they were, the early hunters and miners of gold failed to get it all...or even a large part of it. To the contrary, many competent mining engineers estimate that less than 10% of the gold deposited by nature throughout the West has been recovered. This being so, and even if lots of it is scattered too thinly for profitable mining or is locked up in ores and colloidal deposits, it stands to reason that there are still vast fortunes in gold out there on the deserts and in the mountains...just waiting for a finder.

Why shouldn't it be you!

We now come to the parting, the end of the book...and once again take our separate paths. You cannot help but have learned from the reading; hopefully, you have also enjoyed the hours spent. If, in the final analysis, this little book has only succeeded in sparking your interest in the healthful, exciting hobby of prospecting and panning for gold...it will be worth the price you paid for it. And if, in so doing, it also helps put fresh vigor into your spirit of adventure and brings you into closer contact with your own heritage from the past...it will be worth far more than you can now imagine!

Hasta luego, mi amigo. Vaya siempre con Dios!

Legend:

- MOST PROBABLE PATH OF LARGER PARTICLES AND NUGGETS OF GOLD
- LIKELY LOCATIONS OF SAND AND GRAVEL BUILD-UP
- MAIN FLOW OF MOUNTAIN STREAM

Map labels: BIG NUGGET CREEK, UPPER BONANZA RIVER, LOWER BONANZA RIVER, and elevation contours 6200, 6000, 5800, 5600, 5400, 5200, 5000.

TYPICAL MOUNTAIN STREAM, showing the likely locations of sand and gravel build-up (the yellow areas) along the path of current flow. The dotted black line indicates the most probable pathway that would be taken by the larger particles and nuggets of gold as they are dragged downstream by the power of the flowing water. Obviously, many factors enter into determining actual pathways in any particular stream bed.

THE SLUICE BOX

The purpose of the riffle is to catch gold or other heavy minerals. A properly designed riffle will retard material moving over it, form pockets that retain the gold or other heavy minerals and form eddies to classify the material in the riffle pockets.

There are five broad classifications of riffles.

TRANSVERSE riffle. It is arranged with cross pieces running at a 90 degrees to the water flow in the box bottom. In heavy accumulations of black sand this riffle will tend to pack, but is overcome by frequent clean-ups. A versatile and widely used arrangement is noted for its gold-saving ability and is generally accepted as the best all around riffle. Five examples may be seen in Figure 1 #1,2,3,4,5.

LONGITUDINAL riffle. This riffle is constructed of pieces running in the same direction as the sluice water flows. This riffle is useful for saving course gold, but doesn't function as well in the recovery of the fine gold. So this one is used mainly in the first few sections of a long sluice string. Two examples are shown in Figure 1 #6, #7.

BLOCK riffle. Constructed of 4" x 4" x 8" wooden blocks set on end in the bottom of the sluice, held in place with board strips. These blocks are staggered to keep the gold from escaping between the block joints. This riffle works extremely well in operations where heavy rock is encountered. See Figure 1, example #8.

COBBLE riffle. This riffle is constructed by laying a course of cobble rocks in the bottom of the sluice. Clean-up means taking up and relaying the entire riffle section. Cobble riffles are used in tall sluices that are seldom cleaned up. See Figure 1 #9.

SCREEN AND MATTING riffle This riffle consists of a matting and a heavy mesh 1/4 inch screen. The matting is laid in the bottom of the sluice and the screen is forced down on the matting and securely fastened. This is used at the tail end of a sluice string to catch the very fine gold that failed to settle out in the other riffles. An excellent fine gold saver, and it is highly recommended. See Figure 1 #10.

TRANSVERSE RIFFLES: FIGURE 1

#1   This one is constructed of wooden side rails and steel-capped wooden cross rails. This arrangement is usually known as the Hungarian riffle. The steel caps retard riffle wear and cause a definite water boil. But while the steel strips are beneficial, they are costly and hard to install.

#2   This riffle is constructed in the same manner as the Hungarian riffle, but without the steel caps. This widely used and easily constructed arrangement is known as the cross riffle.

#3   This riffle is constructed of peeled willow poles. This arrangement is the transverse pole riffle. Material may be any round material. It works well, but is not as popular as the transverse which is constructed of square material.

#4   This riffle is constructed of angle iron. It is an excellent riffle,used mainlyfor dredging operations.

#5   This one is constructed of a staggered pattern by nailing wooden strips directly to the bottom of the sluice trough. It works quite well, but difficult to clean. To clean-a complete disassembly of the riffle section is necessary.

LONGITUDINAL RIFFLES: Figure 1

#6   This riffle is constructed of poles and like the pole transverse riffle, may be made of any round material. A good arrangement for coarse gold and is easily constructed.

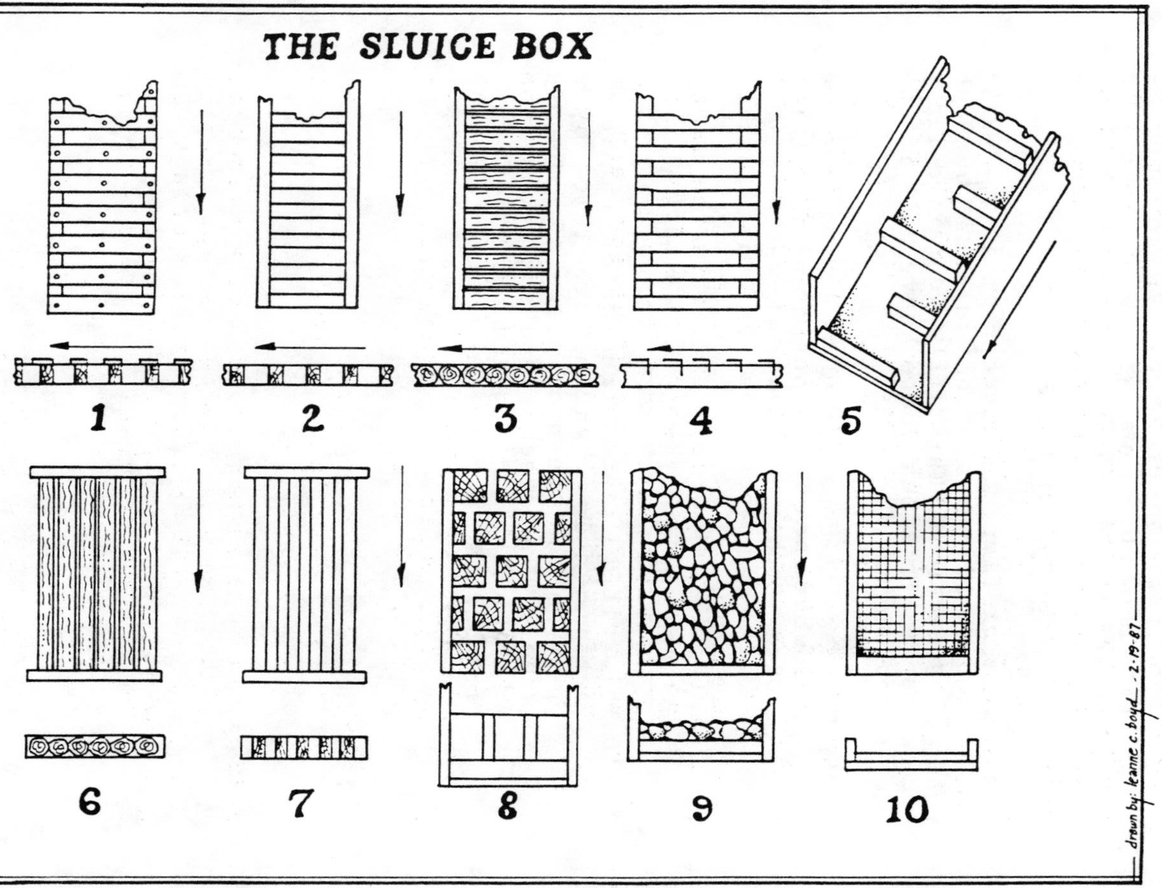

THE SLUICE BOX

FIGURE 1—Varied riffle arrangements.

#7 This riffle is constructed of 1" x 2"
    boards. It is more widely used than the
    longitudinal pole riffle, and seems to do
    a better job of recovery. The riffle
    boards can be capped with steel strips to
    retard riffle wear.

BLOCK RIFFLE: Figure 1

#8 This riffles constructed of 4" x 4" x 8"
    square timber sections or small but-cut
    log sections. Thisriffle is particularly
    useful in areas where heavy rock is en-
    countered

#9 This one is constructed by laying a course
    of cobble rock in the bottom of the sluice
    trough. Cobble riffles work well, but are
    laborious to construct and difficult to
    clean up.

SCREEN AND MATTING RIFFLE: Figure 1

#10 This riffle is constructed of a coarse
    matting held down in the sluice by a
    heavy mesh screen or piece of expanded
    steel. The screen keeps the rocks from
    clogging the matting and retards matting
    wear. This is noted as a good fine gold
    saver.

THE SLUICE BOX

<u>CONSTRUCTION</u> <u>MATERIALS</u> <u>FOR</u> <u>A</u> <u>BASIC</u> <u>SLUICE</u> <u>BOX</u>

To construct the basic sluice the following materials are needed: (remember that planed lumber is narrower than the dimension under which it is sold.)

1 piece-1" x 12" clear pine board8feetlong.
2pieces-1" x 8" clear pineboard 12 feetlong.
3 pieces-1" x 2" clear pine board12 feetlong.
1 piece-1/4 heavy mesh 12 gauge screen 11 5/8" x 48". Expanded metal may be substituted for the screen.
1 piece-carpet, blanket or other coarse matting 11 5/8" x 48".
8-1/4" x 2" carriage bolts, nuts and flat washers.
6-1/4" x 3" carriage bolts, nuts and flat washers.
40-10 x 2" wood screws.
16-1/4" x 1 1/2" lag screws with flat washers.
1/2 pound-#6 cement coated box nails.
small box of small staples.

<u>TOOLS</u> <u>NEEDED:</u>
Hammer, screwdriver, saw, square, adjustable wrench, drill and drill bits (1/4" bit, #10 screw pilot hole bit, 1/2" screw pilot hole bit.

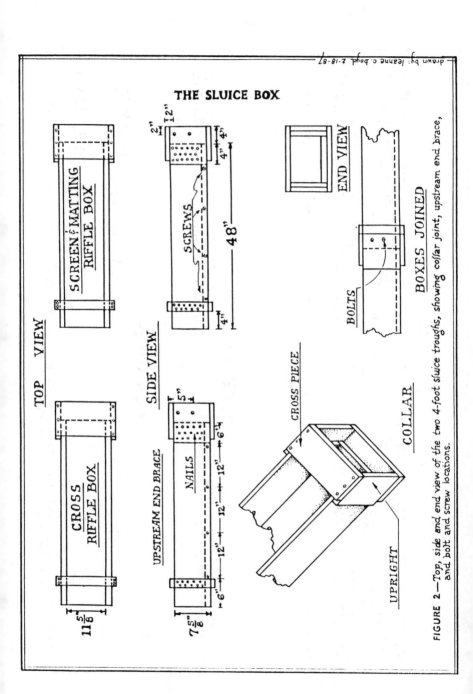

THE SLUICE BOX

FIGURE 2 — Top, side and end view of the two 4-foot sluice troughs, showing collar joint, upstream end brace, and bolt and screw locations.

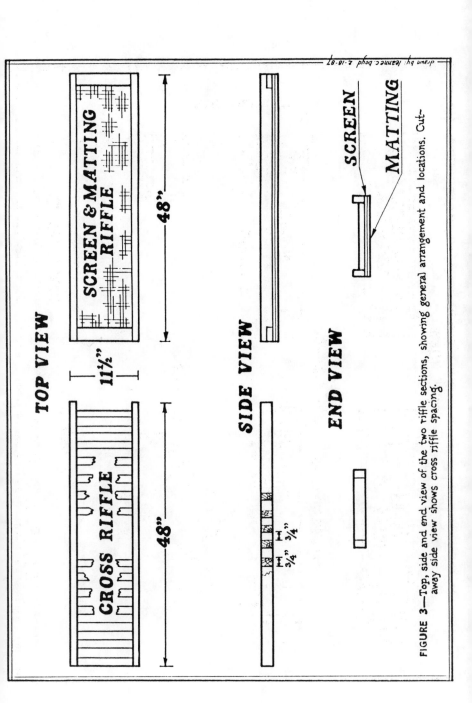

FIGURE 3 —Top, side and end view of the two riffle sections, showing general arrangement and locations. Cut-away side view shows cross riffle spacing.